COOKING WITH
Bon Appétit

COOKING WITH
Bon Appétit

Cakes

THE KNAPP PRESS
Publishers
Los Angeles

Published by The Knapp Press
5900 Wilshire Boulevard, Los Angeles, California 90036

Library of Congress Cataloging in Publication Data

Main entry under title:

Cakes.

  (Cooking with Bon appétit)
  Includes index.
  1. Cake. I. Series.
TX771.C273 1987   641.8'653   87-3969
ISBN 0-89535-180-3

On the cover: *Chocolate Apricot Pecan Torte. Photo by Irwin Horowitz.*

Printed and bound in the United States of America

10   9   8   7   6   5   4

❦ Contents

❧ *Foreword*

It isn't easy to define a word like "cake." It can mean so many things to so many different people. Asked to describe the quintessential cake, you might recall the large, fluffy layer cake that was the magical highlight of childhood birthday parties; or the golden, buttery slices of pound cake topped with strawberries that was served at every summer church social; or the first experience at a fancy French restaurant, when dessert was a rich chocolate gâteau, wonderfully sophisticated yet reassuringly familiar. We serve cakes to welcome guests to our home and to share at informal gatherings. Every important event in our lives, it seems—whether it's a birthday, a wedding or the opening of a new business—is signified by the presence of a great cake.

Cakes come in a multitude of sizes, shapes and flavors. And, depending on their country of origin, they go by a number of different names—*gâteau, torten, kugels* and so on. To bring order out of all this delicious chaos, we have organized this volume of recipes in the following manner: quick cakes, coffee cakes and pound cakes; classic frosted, filled and layered cakes (including rolled cakes); frozen cakes; flourless and nut cakes; and special occasion cakes. Don't be misled by the last category; all the recipes in the book are special in some way. However, these are a bit fancier in presentation and may be more elaborate in preparation.

In addition to many fine recipes—from easy quick loaves you can whip up in one bowl to fancier confections—you will find useful information for adapting standard cake-making methods to the food processor, and tips for creating successful nut cakes.

The great thing about cakes is that they are as much fun to make as they are to eat. Often they require a certain amount of imagination and even expertise, technique that is polished as it is practiced. In this cookbook you will discover plenty of opportunities to perfect your technique, as well as to create some new and memorable cakes.

1 ❦ Quick Cakes, Coffee Cakes and Pound Cakes

In an age when high tech and fast food are a part of everyday life, it's nice to have something that can be prepared quickly, yet at the same time fills the house with the comforting fragrance of home-baked sweets and evokes visions of a slower-paced world. Regardless of whether you use an earthenware bowl and wooden spoon or an ultra-modern food processor to whip them up, the quick cakes and coffee cakes in this chapter are guaranteed to be easy and satisfying.

These dense, moist cakes, unlike the more delicate sponge cakes and génoise, are substantial enough to allow such delicious additions as nuts, fruits, chocolate chips—even vegetables. They range from the simple French Apple Cake (page 2) and Banana Crunch Cake (page 15) to a pretty Strawberry-topped Nut Cake (page 4) and an unusual Chocolate, Prune and Cognac Cake (page 20). Keep in mind that these seldom need any garnish except for perhaps a sprinkling of powdered sugar or a light citrus- or liqueur-spiked glaze. The addition of a little fresh fruit and a dollop of whipped cream can turn even the simplest one into a special dessert.

For many people, a classic cake is a pound cake, so named because it was originally made with one pound each of flour, butter, eggs and sugar. Our versions may be a little lighter on the butter and eggs, but they're every bit as delicious. They range from the basic Old World Sour Cream Pound Cake (page 21) to one made with chocolate chips and currants (page 23) and an English pound cake flavored with chestnuts (page 25). Remember, when making these and other cakes that call for solid shortening, to beat the shortening, sugar and eggs thoroughly, until very light and fluffy. But when you add flour and liquids, mix them gently just until they're combined to ensure a light, tender cake.

Because they're so easy to make, these cakes can be made at the last minute and served warm from the oven. But they are also good because they will keep (when tightly wrapped) about a week at room temperature or several weeks when refrigerated. Of course, they all freeze beautifully, to be brought out and defrosted for a quick dessert. Or enjoy them with a hot cup of coffee or tea on those days when you might need a little extra home-baked comfort.

 Quick Cakes

Acadia Apple Cake

8 to 10 servings

1½ cups all purpose flour
1 cup sugar
2 eggs, beaten until frothy
½ cup vegetable oil
1½ teaspoons vanilla
1 teaspoon cinnamon
1 teaspoon baking soda

½ teaspoon salt
2 cups peeled and finely chopped Golden or Red Delicious apples
1 cup chopped pecans or walnuts
Sweetened whipped cream or vanilla ice cream

Preheat oven to 350°F. Generously grease 9x13-inch baking pan. Mix first 8 ingredients in large bowl. Blend in apples and nuts. Spoon batter into prepared pan, spreading evenly. Bake until toothpick inserted in center comes out clean, 25 to 30 minutes. Serve warm with whipped cream or ice cream.

French Apple Cake

8 servings

3 large eggs
6 tablespoons sugar
10 tablespoons (1¼ sticks) butter, melted
11 tablespoons all purpose flour

1 tablespoon baking powder
5 cups peeled Golden Delicious apples cut into ½-inch chunks
2 tablespoons light rum
Powdered sugar

Preheat oven to 350°F. Butter 10-inch springform pan. Using electric mixer, beat eggs and sugar until light and fluffy. Beat in melted butter. Mix flour and baking powder in small bowl. Add to egg mixture and blend just until flour is moistened. Stir in apples and rum. Immediately pour into prepared pan. Bake until golden brown and tester inserted in center comes out clean, 30 to 35 minutes. Cool to room temperature. Sprinkle with powdered sugar.

Applesauce Spice Cake

12 to 16 servings

2½ cups all purpose flour
2 cups sugar
2 cups applesauce
½ cup solid vegetable shortening, room temperature
½ cup water
2 eggs, beaten to blend
1½ teaspoons baking powder
1½ teaspoons baking soda
1 teaspoon vanilla

1 teaspoon salt
1 teaspoon cinnamon
½ teaspoon ground cloves
½ teaspoon ground allspice
½ teaspoon freshly grated nutmeg
1 cup chopped walnuts
1 cup raisins
Vanilla Frosting*
Walnut halves

Preheat oven to 350°F. Grease and flour two 9-inch round baking pans. Combine all ingredients except walnuts, raisins and frosting in large bowl of electric mixer and beat well. Stir in chopped walnuts and raisins. Turn into pans, spreading evenly. Bake until golden brown and toothpick inserted in centers comes out clean, 30 to 35 minutes. Cool completely. Spread frosting between layers and over top and sides. Arrange nuts around bottom of cake.

*Vanilla Frosting

Makes about 3¼ cups

¾ cup (1½ sticks) butter, room temperature	¼ cup milk
	2 teaspoons vanilla
5 cups sifted powdered sugar	

Using electric mixer, beat butter in small bowl until light and fluffy, 3 to 4 minutes. Add remaining ingredients and beat until smooth, about 3 minutes.

Buttermilk-glazed Carrot Cake

To save time, shred the carrots and chop the walnuts in the food processor.

10 to 12 servings

2 cups all purpose flour	½ cup vegetable oil
1½ cups sugar	2 teaspoons vanilla
2 teaspoons cinnamon	2 cups finely shredded peeled carrots
1 teaspoon baking soda	1 8-ounce can crushed pineapple, drained
½ teaspoon salt	
¾ cup buttermilk	1 cup chopped walnuts
3 eggs, beaten to blend	Buttermilk Glaze*

Preheat oven to 350°F. Combine first 5 ingredients in medium bowl. Stir together buttermilk, eggs, oil and vanilla in large bowl. Add dry ingredients and stir until well blended. Mix in carrots, pineapple and walnuts. Pour batter into 9x13-inch ovenproof glass baking dish. Bake until tester inserted in center comes out clean, about 45 minutes. Cool cake. Drizzle with hot Buttermilk Glaze. Let glaze cool slightly before serving carrot cake.

*Buttermilk Glaze

Makes about 1¼ cups

⅔ cup sugar	2 tablespoons light corn syrup
⅓ cup butter, melted	¼ teaspoon baking soda
⅓ cup buttermilk	½ teaspoon vanilla

Combine first 5 ingredients in heavy medium saucepan. Bring to boil over medium heat, stirring frequently. Boil until slightly thickened, about 5 minutes. Remove from heat. Stir in vanilla. Use glaze immediately.

Zucchini Lemon-Almond Tea Cake

A light cake to enjoy after dinner or with iced tea or lemonade.

8 to 10 servings

2 cups finely shredded zucchini	¼ cup fresh lemon juice
1 teaspoon salt	2 tablespoons grated lemon peel
	2¼ cups all purpose flour
1 cup vegetable oil	2 teaspoons baking soda
¾ cup sugar	½ teaspoon baking powder
3 eggs, room temperature	1½ cups chopped almonds
½ cup honey	2 tablespoons honey

Mix zucchini and salt in colander. Weight with plate and let drain 1 hour. Squeeze out excess moisture.

Preheat oven to 350°F. Grease 9x13-inch glass baking dish. Mix oil, sugar, eggs, ½ cup honey, lemon juice and peel in large bowl until well blended. Mix in zucchini. Sift flour, baking soda and baking powder; stir into zucchini. Fold in nuts. Pour into prepared dish. Bake until cake is springy to touch, about 35 minutes. Spread 2 tablespoons honey over top. Cool in pan. Serve at room temperature.

Papaya Cake

12 servings

3 cups all purpose flour
2 teaspoons baking soda
1 teaspoon cinnamon
½ teaspoon salt
½ teaspoon freshly grated nutmeg
¼ teaspoon ground ginger
½ cup solid vegetable shortening

1½ cups sugar
2 eggs
2 tablespoons water
1 teaspoon fresh lemon juice
2 cups diced papaya
1 cup golden raisins
Powdered sugar

Preheat oven to 350°F. Grease and flour 2-quart brioche pan or 9x13x2-inch baking pan, shaking out excess. Mix flour, baking soda, cinnamon, salt, nutmeg and ginger. Cream shortening with sugar in large bowl of electric mixer. Beat in eggs one at a time. Stir in flour mixture. Add water and lemon juice and blend well. Fold in papaya and raisins. Pour batter into prepared pan. Bake until tester inserted in center comes out clean, about 1¼ hours in brioche pan or 45 minutes in rectangular pan. Let cake cool in pan on wire rack. Turn cake out onto platter. Dust with sugar before serving.

Quick Strawberry Cake

6 to 8 servings

3 cups fresh strawberries, sliced
5 tablespoons fresh orange juice
1¼ cups sugar
1 cup all purpose flour
½ cup milk
3 tablespoons butter, melted

1 teaspoon baking powder
¼ teaspoon salt
1 tablespoon cornstarch
1 teaspoon vanilla
1 cup boiling water
Vanilla ice cream

Preheat oven to 350°F. Butter 9-inch square baking dish. Arrange strawberries in bottom. Pour orange juice over. Combine 1 cup sugar, flour, milk, butter, baking powder and salt in large bowl and blend until smooth. Spread over strawberries. Mix remaining ¼ cup sugar, cornstarch and vanilla. Sprinkle over batter. Carefully pour boiling water over batter. Bake until golden brown, about 50 minutes. Let stand 5 minutes. Serve with ice cream.

Strawberry-topped Nut Cake

8 servings

4 eggs, beaten to blend
1 cup sugar
1⅓ cups walnuts, ground
6 tablespoons all purpose flour
1 teaspoon baking powder

1 teaspoon vanilla
½ cup strawberry jam

½ cup sifted powdered sugar
1 tablespoon fresh orange juice

Preheat oven to 350°F. Grease 9-inch springform pan. Beat eggs and 1 cup sugar in large bowl of electric mixer until pale yellow and slowly dissolving ribbon forms when beaters are lifted, about 4 minutes. Blend in ground nuts, flour, baking powder and vanilla on low speed until well combined. Pour batter into prepared pan. Bake until tester inserted in center comes out clean, about 30 minutes. Cool 10 minutes. Spread jam over. Cool completely.

Remove pan edges. Mix powdered sugar and orange juice until sugar dissolves and glaze is smooth. Drizzle over cake and down sides, allowing some jam to show through. Let stand at least 1 hour or overnight. Serve at room temperature.

Almond Morning Cake

10 to 12 servings

1 envelope dry yeast
⅓ cup warm water (105°F to 115°F)
1 cup blanched almonds
3 eggs
1½ cups self-rising flour

¾ cup sugar
½ cup (1 stick) butter, cut up, room temperature
1 teaspoon almond extract
Powdered sugar

Preheat oven to 350°F. Lightly grease 10-inch springform pan. Combine yeast and water in small bowl and stir until dissolved. Set aside. Chop almonds in processor using on/off turns. Add eggs, flour, sugar, butter, almond extract and yeast mixture and blend thoroughly. Pour batter into prepared pan. Bake until golden, about 30 to 40 minutes. Cool in pan 30 minutes. Transfer cake to platter. Dust top with powdered sugar before serving.

Brandy Almond Cake

This is great served with ice cream, sauces or fruit.

Makes one 9x5-inch loaf

⅓ cup sliced almonds
½ cup (1 stick) plus 3 tablespoons butter, room temperature
⅔ cup sugar
7 ounces almond paste, cut into small pieces, room temperature
2 eggs, room temperature
3 tablespoons milk, room temperature

1 tablespoon brandy *or* 1 teaspoon vanilla
1½ cups all purpose flour
1½ teaspoons baking powder
¼ teaspoon salt
3 tablespoons sliced almonds

Preheat oven to 350°F. Butter 9x5-inch loaf pan. Sprinkle bottom of pan with ⅓ cup sliced almonds, shaking to coat evenly. Set pan aside.

Cream butter in large bowl of electric mixer at high speed until fluffy. Gradually beat in sugar. Beat in almond paste one piece at a time until mixture is smooth and nearly white, at least 10 minutes. Beat in eggs one at a time. Blend in milk and brandy.

Sift in dry ingredients and blend at low speed just until incorporated. Turn batter into prepared pan. Sprinkle with remaining 3 tablespoons almonds. Bake until tester inserted in center comes out clean, about 1 hour. Cool cake in pan on rack.

🍒 *Adapting to the Food Processor*

Sifting, creaming, folding, blending, stirring and beating—steps frequently required in cake preparation—can be quickly and efficiently accomplished with the help of a food processor. With the basic steps and techniques that follow, delectable results can be achieved in record time.

Basic Steps

Using the steel knife, process the dry ingredients for 3 seconds to mix, then set aside. Slice or chop fruit or nuts as required. Set aside. Mix sugar and eggs one minute. Add butter or oil and mix one minute. Add liquid and flavoring and mix just until blended. Add dry ingredients and mix using on/off turns just until flour is incorporated.

Tips and Techniques

- When a recipe requires separately beaten egg whites, process them first in a clean, dry work bowl. Egg whites processed with 2 teaspoons distilled white vinegar whip into a medium-firm texture that holds up well while cake batter is processed. Gently transfer them from work bowl to mixing bowl. It is not necessary to wash work bowl before proceeding.

- When processing eggs or egg yolks with sugar, the color of the mixture will lighten as it becomes fluffy and smooth. Stop once to scrape down sides of work bowl. Use steel knife.

- Softened shortening, butter or margarine is placed on top of the batter in pieces, but oil is poured slowly through the feed tube while machine is running. Use steel knife.

- To melt chocolate in processor, heat liquid and keep at simmer. Break chocolate into pieces and mix with sugar until chocolate is as fine as sugar. With machine running, pour hot liquid through feed tube and mix until chocolate is completely melted, stopping once to scrape down sides and cover of work bowl. Use steel knife.

- Other liquid ingredients—milk, cream, buttermilk, water, juice or flavorings—are poured through feed tube while machine is running. To add sour cream or yogurt, stop machine, spoon into work bowl and then blend thoroughly. Use steel knife.

- To pour batter easily without removal of the steel knife, secure the knife in place from underneath with your finger. After most of the batter is transferred, replace work bowl and steel knife on machine base. Pulse once (or use on/off turns); the batter will spin onto the sides of work bowl for easy removal with a spatula.

Graham Nut Cake

Makes one 9x5-inch loaf

3 eggs, room temperature
2¼ cups fine graham cracker crumbs
1½ cups chopped walnuts or pecans
1½ cups flaked coconut
1 cup milk

¾ cup sugar
½ cup (1 stick) butter, melted and
  cooled completely
1 teaspoon baking powder

Preheat oven to 250°F. Butter and flour 9x5-inch loaf pan. Beat eggs in large bowl until light and fluffy. Stir in all remaining ingredients using wooden spoon. Turn batter into prepared pan. Bake until edges are lightly browned and tester inserted in center comes out clean, about 1 hour and 35 minutes. Cool in pan 10 minutes. Invert onto rack and cool completely.

Orange Walnut Cake

10 servings

All purpose flour

2½ cups cake flour
1 cup walnuts, lightly toasted
1 tablespoon baking powder
¾ teaspoon baking soda
½ teaspoon ground cloves
½ teaspoon freshly grated nutmeg
¼ teaspoon salt

4 teaspoons grated orange peel
1½ cups sugar
3 eggs
1¼ cups vegetable oil
½ cup orange juice concentrate,
  thawed
½ cup plain yogurt

Orange Glaze*

Position rack in center of oven and preheat to 350°F. Generously butter 12-cup bundt or tube pan; dust lightly with flour.

In processor mix cake flour, walnuts, baking powder, baking soda, cloves, nutmeg and salt until nuts are coarsely chopped, about 5 seconds. Set aside.

Finely mince orange peel with sugar. Add eggs and blend 1 minute, stopping once to scrape down sides of work bowl. With machine running, pour oil through feed tube and mix 1 minute. Add orange juice concentrate and yogurt and blend 10 seconds. Add dry ingredients to work bowl. Mix until ingredients are just combined, using several on/off turns.

Transfer batter to prepared pan. Stir through with knife to release air bubbles. Bake cake until tester inserted in center comes out clean, 50 to 55 minutes. Cool in pan 5 minutes. Invert onto rack set on baking sheet. Turn cake right side up. Immediately spoon glaze slowly over top of cake, allowing some to drizzle down sides. Cool completely before serving. *(Can be prepared 3 days ahead.)*

*Orange Glaze

Makes about 1 cup

2 cups powdered sugar
3 tablespoons orange juice
  concentrate, thawed

2 tablespoons water
½ teaspoon vanilla
Pinch of salt

Blend all ingredients in processor or blender until smooth, stopping occasionally to scrape down sides of container.

Fruit-filled Ricotta and Rum Cake

12 servings

Butter
All purpose flour
3 cups all purpose flour
2 teaspoons baking powder
½ teaspoon salt
2 cups sugar
5 eggs, room temperature
1 cup vegetable oil
1 cup (8 ounces) ricotta cheese
1 tablespoon grated orange peel

2 teaspoons vanilla
2 tablespoons dark rum
1 cup papaya jelly or apricot preserves, heated and strained

3 cups cut-up fruit (such as mango, papaya, banana, strawberries, kiwis and raspberries)
¼ cup dark rum
Sugar

Position rack in center of oven and preheat to 350°F. Butter 12-cup bundt or tube pan and dust with flour. Sift 3 cups flour, baking powder and salt together 2 times. Using electric mixer, gradually beat 2 cups sugar into eggs. Continue beating until pale yellow and slowly dissolving ribbon forms when beaters are lifted. Combine oil, ricotta, orange peel, vanilla and 2 tablespoons rum. Add to eggs, mixing on low speed. Sift flour mixture onto batter in 3 additions, folding until just combined. Pour batter into pan. Bake until cake pulls away from sides of pan and center is springy to touch, about 1¼ hours. Cool on rack 15 minutes. Invert cake onto platter. Brush papaya jelly onto warm cake. Cool to room temperature.

Combine fruit with ¼ cup rum and sugar to taste. Just before serving, spoon fruit mixture into center of cake.

Grenadian Spice Cake

As rich as a pound cake, this dessert does not require icing.

Makes one 9x5-inch loaf

2 cups all purpose flour, sifted
½ teaspoon baking powder
⅛ teaspoon salt
1½ cups sugar
1 cup (2 sticks) unsalted butter, well chilled and cut into tablespoon-size pieces
1½ teaspoons finely grated lime peel

1 teaspoon freshly grated nutmeg
½ teaspoon cinnamon
¼ teaspoon ground allspice
3 large eggs, room temperature
½ cup milk, room temperature

Sliced fresh fruit (garnish)

Preheat oven to 350°F. Grease and flour 9x5-inch loaf pan, shaking out excess flour. Set aside.

Resift 2 cups flour with baking powder and salt and set aside. Combine sugar, butter, lime peel, nutmeg, cinnamon and allspice in large bowl of electric mixer and beat on high speed until light, about 5 minutes. Reduce mixer speed to medium and blend in eggs one at a time, mixing thoroughly. Add sifted dry ingredients to batter alternately with milk, beginning and ending with dry ingredients.

Spoon batter into prepared pan, pushing into corners and smoothing top. Bake until tester inserted near center of cake comes out clean, about 1¼ to 1½ hours. Cool cake upright in pan on wire rack 10 minutes; loosen edges with thin-blade spatula and turn cake out onto wire rack. Cool to room temperature. Garnish with fresh fruit.

Double Ginger Gingerbread

8 servings

2 cups sifted unbleached all purpose flour
1½ teaspoons cinnamon
1 teaspoon ground ginger
1 teaspoon baking powder
½ teaspoon baking soda
¼ teaspoon salt
⅛ teaspoon ground cardamom
⅛ teaspoon ground cloves
½ cup (1 stick) unsalted butter, room temperature

½ cup firmly packed dark brown sugar
1 egg
¾ cup light molasses
¾ cup buttermilk
3 tablespoons minced crystallized ginger
1 tablespoon grated orange peel
Grand Marnier Cream*

Position rack in center of oven and preheat to 350°F. Grease 8-inch square baking pan; dust with flour. Sift first 8 ingredients into bowl. Using electric mixer, cream butter in another bowl. Add brown sugar and beat until light and fluffy. Beat in egg, then molasses. Mix in buttermilk alternately with dry ingredients. Fold in crystallized ginger and orange peel. Spoon batter into prepared pan. Bake until springy to touch, 45 to 50 minutes. Cool cake in pan on rack. Serve with cream.

*Grand Marnier Cream

Makes about 2 cups

⅔ cup well-chilled whipping cream
2 teaspoons Grand Marnier
1 teaspoon vanilla

3 tablespoons sugar
3 tablespoons sour cream

Beat cream, Grand Marnier and vanilla until beginning to thicken. Add sugar and sour cream and beat until soft peaks form. Serve immediately.

Whole-Grain Pineapple Spice Cake

8 servings

4 cups water
8 ounces dried pineapple, cut into ¼-inch dice

1¼ cups corn oil
1 cup sugar
½ cup firmly packed light brown sugar
4 eggs
1 cup unbleached all purpose flour
½ cup whole wheat flour, preferably stone-ground

½ cup medium rye flour
1 tablespoon baking powder
1 teaspoon salt
1 teaspoon cinnamon
½ teaspoon freshly grated nutmeg
¼ teaspoon ground ginger
¼ teaspoon ground allspice
¼ teaspoon ground cloves
1 cup coarsely chopped pecans
Pineapple Rum Glaze*

Bring water to boil. Pour over pineapple. Cool completely. Drain.

Position rack in center of oven and preheat to 350°F. Butter and flour 10-cup ring pan, shaking out excess. Whisk oil and sugars in large bowl. Whisk in eggs one at a time. Combine flours, baking powder, salt and spices in another bowl. Add pineapple, dry ingredients and pecans into egg mixture and stir just to combine. Pour batter into prepared pan. Bake until puffed, golden and pulls away from sides of pan, 50 to 60 minutes. Cool 10 minutes in pan on rack. Invert cake onto platter. Cool completely. Drizzle with Pineapple Rum Glaze.

*Pineapple Rum Glaze

Makes about ¾ cup

⅓ cup pineapple juice
¼ cup (½ stick) unsalted butter
¼ cup sugar

¼ cup firmly packed light brown
  sugar
¼ cup dark rum

Combine all ingredients in heavy small saucepan over medium heat and bring to boil, stirring occasionally. Reduce heat and simmer briskly until bubbly and caramel colored, about 7 minutes. Cool to room temperature.

Spiced Whiskey Cake

10 to 12 servings

2¼ cups cake flour
1 tablespoon baking powder
1 teaspoon baking soda
1 teaspoon ground ginger
1 teaspoon cinnamon
½ teaspoon ground cardamom
½ teaspoon ground allspice
½ teaspoon ground cloves
¼ teaspoon salt

1½ cups sugar
2 eggs
1 cup (2 sticks) unsalted butter, cut
  into 8 pieces, room temperature
¾ cup buttermilk
½ cup bourbon

Bourbon Glaze*

Position rack in center of oven and preheat to 350°F. Generously butter 12-cup bundt or tube pan. Set aside.

Blend first 9 ingredients in processor 3 seconds. Set aside. Mix sugar and eggs 1 minute, stopping once to scrape down sides of work bowl. Add butter and blend 1 minute. With machine running, pour buttermilk and bourbon through feed tube and mix 10 seconds. Add dry ingredients to work bowl and mix using 2 on/off turns. Run spatula around inside of work bowl to loosen mixture. Blend until ingredients are just combined, using 1 or 2 on/off turns.

Transfer batter to prepared pan. Stir through with knife to release air bubbles. Bake until tester inserted in center comes out clean, 40 to 45 minutes. Cool in pan on rack 10 minutes. Invert cake onto rack set on baking sheet. Slowly spoon glaze over top of hot cake, allowing some to melt down sides and making sure all glaze is incorporated into cake. Serve warm or at room temperature. *(Can be prepared 3 days ahead. Store at room temperature.)*

*Bourbon Glaze

Makes about ½ cup

1 cup plus 2 tablespoons powdered
  sugar
2 tablespoons (¼ stick) unsalted
  butter, halved, room temperature

2 tablespoons bourbon
1½ tablespoons vanilla

Mix all ingredients in processor or blender until smooth, about 10 seconds, stopping once to scrape down sides of bowl.

Carob Bundt Cake

10 to 12 servings

3 cups all purpose flour
¾ cup powdered roasted carob*
2 teaspoons baking soda
2 teaspoons baking powder
½ teaspoon salt
2 cups sugar
1 cup vegetable oil
2 eggs, beaten to blend
1 cup water
1 cup milk

1 teaspoon vanilla
1 8-ounce package cream cheese, room temperature
¼ cup sugar
6 ounces carob chips
½ cup shredded unsweetened coconut
1 teaspoon vanilla
   Powdered sugar

Preheat oven to 375°F. Lightly butter 6-cup bundt pan. Sift flour, powdered carob, baking soda, baking powder and salt into medium bowl. Combine 2 cups sugar with oil in another bowl. Stir in eggs. Add flour mixture and blend thoroughly. Mix in water, milk and 1 teaspoon vanilla. Set batter aside.

   Blend cream cheese with ¼ cup sugar in medium bowl. Mix in carob chips, coconut and vanilla. Pour half of cake batter into prepared pan. Top with cream cheese filling. Add remaining batter to pan. Bake until center of cake is firm to touch, about 60 minutes. Cool in pan 10 minutes. Invert onto rack and cool completely. Dust cake with powdered sugar before serving.

*Powdered roasted carob is available at natural foods stores.

Wacky Cake

16 servings

1½ cups unbleached all purpose flour
1½ cups sugar
⅓ cup unsweetened cocoa powder
1 teaspoon baking soda
1 teaspoon salt
1 cup warm water
3 teaspoons vanilla

⅓ cup vegetable oil
1 teaspoon distilled white vinegar
¼ cup (½ stick) butter
2 tablespoons milk
2 tablespoons unsweetened cocoa powder

Preheat oven to 350°F. Sift flour, 1 cup sugar, ⅓ cup cocoa powder, baking soda and salt into 8-inch square pan. Make three 2-inch holes in flour mixture with fork. Pour warm water and 1 teaspoon vanilla into 1 hole. Pour oil into another. Pour vinegar into third. Stir through batter until well mixed, 1 to 2 minutes. Bake until toothpick inserted in center comes out clean, about 30 minutes. Cool cake completely in pan.

   Combine remaining ½ cup sugar, butter, milk and 2 tablespoons cocoa powder in small saucepan over medium heat and bring to boil. Reduce heat and simmer 1 minute. Remove from heat and stir until cool, about 5 minutes. Add remaining 2 teaspoons vanilla and mix well. Spread icing over cake in pan. Let cool until set.

Zucchini Chocolate Cake

12 servings

1⅓ cups sugar
½ cup (1 stick) butter, room temperature
½ cup vegetable oil

½ cup milk
1 teaspoon fresh lemon juice
2 eggs
1 teaspoon vanilla
2½ cups all purpose flour

6 tablespoons unsweetened cocoa powder
1 teaspoon baking soda
½ teaspoon cinnamon
½ teaspoon baking powder
Pinch of salt
2 cups grated zucchini
Powdered sugar

Preheat oven to 325°F. Grease and flour 9x13-inch baking pan. Mix sugar, butter and oil in large bowl. Combine milk and lemon juice in small bowl and add to sugar mixture. Add eggs and vanilla and blend well. Sift together flour and cocoa. Add baking soda, cinnamon, baking powder and salt to dry ingredients and blend well. Stir into sugar mixture. Mix in zucchini. Pour into prepared pan. Bake until tester inserted in center comes out clean, about 40 minutes. Cool to room temperature. Sprinkle top with powdered sugar before serving.

Shirley's Chocolate Brownie Cake

16 servings

1½ cups all purpose flour
1 cup sugar
¾ cup water
⅓ cup vegetable oil
1 egg, beaten to blend
2 ounces unsweetened chocolate, melted

½ teaspoon vanilla
½ teaspoon salt
½ teaspoon baking powder
1 cup semisweet chocolate chips
½ cup chopped walnuts

Preheat over to 350°F. Combine first 9 ingredients in 8-inch square baking pan and mix until smooth. Sprinkle with chocolate chips and walnuts. Bake until toothpick inserted in center comes out clean, about 30 minutes. Cool cake completely. Cut into squares to serve.

 Coffee Cakes

Swedish Cardamom Cake

8 to 10 servings

Butter
Vanilla wafer crumbs
2 cups all purpose flour
1¼ cups sugar
2 teaspoons baking powder

1 teaspoon cardamom seed, ground
½ teaspoon salt
3 eggs, room temperature
1½ cups whipping cream
Powdered sugar

Preheat oven to 350°F. Butter 9-inch kugelhopf mold or tube pan. Coat with wafer crumbs. Combine flour, 1¼ cups sugar, baking powder, cardamom and salt in large bowl of electric mixer. Blend in eggs and cream on low speed. Beat at medium speed until batter is texture of softly whipped cream. Pour into prepared pan. Bake until toothpick inserted in center comes out clean, about 55 minutes. Remove cake from pan. Cool completely on rack. Before serving, dust lightly with powdered sugar.

Maple Pecan Cake

10 servings

¾ cup pure maple syrup
¼ cup (½ stick) unsalted butter
¼ cup firmly packed dark brown sugar
Pinch of ground mace
1¾ cups coarsely chopped pecans

2½ cups bleached all purpose flour
1 teaspoon baking soda
Pinch of salt

½ cup (1 stick) unsalted butter, room temperature
¾ cup sugar
2 eggs, room temperature
1 teaspoon vanilla
1 teaspoon grated lemon peel
1 cup plain yogurt
¾ cup dried currants
Whipped cream (optional)

Generously butter 10-inch-diameter cake pan with high sides (or 7½x11½-inch ovenproof glass baking dish). Heat syrup, ¼ cup butter, brown sugar and mace in heavy medium saucepan over low heat, stirring until sugar dissolves. Bring to boil. Pour into prepared pan. Sprinkle with pecans.

Position rack in center of oven and preheat to 350°F. Sift flour, baking soda and salt into bowl. Using electric mixer, cream ½ cup butter in another bowl. Add ¾ cup sugar and beat until light and fluffy. Beat in eggs 1 at a time, then beat 2 minutes. Blend in vanilla and lemon peel. Stir in flour mixture and yogurt alternately, beginning and ending with flour mixture. Fold in currants. Spoon batter atop pecan mixture, spreading gently to sides of pan. Bake until tester inserted in center comes out clean, about 55 minutes. Immediately invert cake onto rack set over sheet of waxed paper. Serve warm. Pass cream if desired.

Almond Bundkuchen

Large and dramatic, this cake is perfect for a special brunch or breakfast.

16 servings

¾ cup milk
1 cup golden raisins
½ cup currants
1 package dry yeast
1 teaspoon sugar
¼ cup warm water (105°F to 115°F)

6 cups all purpose flour

1 cup (2 sticks) unsalted butter, room temperature

¾ cup sugar
8 eggs, room temperature
2 tablespoons dark rum
1½ tablespoons grated lemon peel
½ teaspoon salt

½ cup chopped toasted sliced almonds

3 tablespoons powdered sugar
3 tablespoons cinnamon

Scald milk in heavy medium saucepan. Stir in raisins and currants. Cool to warm (105°F to 115°F).

Sprinkle yeast and 1 teaspoon sugar over warm water in medium bowl; stir to dissolve. Let stand until foamy and proofed, about 5 minutes.

Strain cooled milk into yeast mixture, reserving fruit. Stir in 1 cup flour. Cover mixture and let rise in warm draft-free area until dough is almost doubled in volume, about 30 minutes.

Cream butter with ¾ cup sugar in large bowl of heavy-duty mixer fitted with dough hook until smooth. Beat in eggs 1 at a time and continue beating until mixture is light and fluffy. Mix in rum, lemon peel and salt. Blend in yeast mixture. Gradually add remaining flour and beat until smooth and satiny, about 1 minute. (Dough can also be prepared with standard electric mixer or by hand.) Stir in reserved golden raisins and currants.

Butter 10- to 12-cup tube or bundt pan. Spoon in half of dough. Sprinkle with almonds. Cover with remaining dough. Cover and let rise in warm draft-free area until dough comes to rim of pan, 1 to 1½ hours.

Preheat oven to 350°F. Bake until cake is golden brown and sounds hollow when tapped on bottom, 50 to 60 minutes. Cool 5 minutes in pan. Invert onto rack and cool completely. Mix powdered sugar and cinnamon. Sprinkle over cake. *(Can be prepared several days ahead and refrigerated, or several weeks ahead and frozen.)*

Orange-Almond Streusel Buttermilk Cake

12 to 14 servings

Streusel
1½ cups chopped toasted almonds
¾ cup finely packed light brown sugar
2 tablespoons grated orange peel
1 teaspoon cinnamon
½ teaspoon mace

Cake
2 tablespoons (¼ stick) unsalted butter, room temperature
3½ cups sifted unbleached all purpose flour

4 teaspoons baking powder
1¼ teaspoons baking soda
½ teaspoon salt
1⅓ cups buttermilk
1½ teaspoons vanilla
1½ cups (3 sticks) unsalted butter, room temperature
2 cups sugar
3 eggs, room temperature
2 teaspoons grated orange peel

For streusel: Blend all ingredients in processor until nuts are chopped medium-fine. Remove all but 1 cup mixture. Finely grind remaining cup.

For cake: Position rack in lower third of oven and preheat to 375°F. Butter 3-quart bundt pan with 2 tablespoons butter. Sprinkle with finely ground streusel. Sift flour, baking powder, baking soda and salt into bowl. Mix buttermilk and vanilla in measuring cup. Using electric mixer, cream 1½ cups butter. Add sugar and beat until light and fluffy. Beat in eggs 1 at a time, then beat 2 minutes. Add orange peel. Mix in dry ingredients and buttermilk alternately, beginning and ending with dry ingredients. Spread ⅓ of batter in prepared pan. Sprinkle with ⅓ of remaining streusel. Using knife, swirl streusel into batter slightly. Repeat layering and swirling twice. Bake until tester inserted in center comes out clean, covering top with foil if cake is browning too quickly, about 55 minutes. Immediately invert cake onto rack. Allow to cool completely before serving.

Toskakake

Claimed by both the Danes and Norwegians, this caramel- and almond-topped cake is a favorite in all the Scandinavian countries.

10 servings

Cake
- 3 eggs, room temperature
- 1 cup sugar
- 1½ cups all purpose flour
- 1½ teaspoons baking powder
- ¾ cup (1½ sticks) unsalted butter, melted
- 3 tablespoons milk
- 1 teaspoon vanilla

Toska Topping
- ⅓ cup unsalted butter
- ½ cup sugar
- ½ cup whipping cream
- ½ cup slivered blanched almonds, toasted

For cake: Position rack in center of oven and preheat to 350°F. Butter 10-inch springform pan. Beat eggs and sugar in medium bowl until pale yellow and slowly dissolving ribbon forms when beaters are lifted, about 6 minutes. Combine flour and baking powder and fold into egg mixture. Fold in melted butter, milk and vanilla until smooth. Turn into prepared pan. Bake until tester inserted in center comes out clean, 30 to 35 minutes.

Just before cake is done, prepare topping: Melt butter in heavy 8-inch skillet over low heat. Mix in sugar and cream and cook, swirling pan occasionally, until sugar dissolves. Increase heat to high and bring to boil. Let mixture boil vigorously exactly 2½ minutes.

Immediately pour hot topping over cake. Sprinkle with nuts. Continue baking until topping is bubbly and brown, watching carefully, about 12 minutes. Cool on rack. Serve warm or at room temperature.

Banana Crunch Cake

Makes one 9x5-inch loaf

Banana Crunch
- 1½ tablespoons butter
- 2 tablespoons honey
- 1 tablespoon sugar
- ½ cup banana chips*

Batter
- ½ cup (1 stick) butter, room temperature
- ¾ cup sugar
- 2 eggs, room temperature
- 1 tablespoon fresh lemon juice

- 1 teaspoon vanilla
- 1½ cups all purpose flour
- 2 tablespoons cultured buttermilk powder
- ¾ teaspoon freshly grated nutmeg
- ¼ teaspoon baking powder
- ¼ teaspoon baking soda
- ¼ teaspoon salt
- ¼ cup banana liqueur
- ¼ cup milk, room temperature

For banana crunch: Butter 9-inch baking pan. Melt 1½ tablespoons butter in heavy small skillet over low heat. Remove skillet from heat and stir in honey and sugar. Return to heat and stir gently until sugar dissolves, about 4 minutes. Continue stirring 1 minute. Add banana chips and stir constantly until golden brown, 7 to 8 minutes. Pour into prepared pan. Cool, then refrigerate uncovered until hard.

When hard, break into small pieces. Finely chop in processor, blender or by hand. Do not pulverize.

For batter: Preheat oven to 350°F. Butter and flour 9x5-inch loaf pan. Cream ½ cup butter in large bowl of electric mixer until fluffy. Gradually beat in sugar. Beat in eggs one at a time. Blend in lemon juice and vanilla. Sift together dry ingredients. Add alternately to batter with liqueur and milk, stirring well after each addition. Fold in banana crunch mixture. Pour into prepared pan. Bake until tester inserted in center comes out clean, 55 minutes. Cool in pan on rack.

*Available at natural foods stores.

Carrot Kuchen

Moist and flavorful, this colorful cake keeps well for several days.

8 to 10 servings

4 eggs, room temperature
1 cup sugar
9 ounces blanched almonds, toasted and finely ground
1½ cups very finely shredded carrots
1 cup all purpose flour

1 teaspoon baking powder
1 cup thick-cut orange marmalade
¼ cup dark rum
Powdered sugar
Grated chocolate
Whipped cream

Preheat oven to 350°F. Butter a 9-inch springform pan. Using electric mixer, beat eggs and sugar in large bowl until thick and light. Fold in almonds and carrots. Mix flour with baking powder, then fold into carrot mixture. Pour into prepared pan. Bake until tester inserted in center comes out clean, about 45 minutes. Cool in pan on rack.

Cut cake in half horizontally using long serrated knife. Set 1 cake layer on platter. Blend marmalade and rum. Spread cake with half of mixture. Top with second cake layer. Spread with remaining marmalade mixture. Pat edges with powdered sugar. Sprinkle outside edge of top with grated chocolate. Serve with whipped cream.

Cranberry Upside-down Marmalade Cake

8 servings

Topping
1 cup firmly packed light brown sugar
6 tablespoons (¾ stick) unsalted butter
½ teaspoon cinnamon
¼ teaspoon freshly grated nutmeg
1 12-ounce package cranberries

Cake
2 cups sifted unbleached all purpose flour

1 teaspoon baking soda
½ teaspoon freshly grated nutmeg
½ teaspoon cinnamon
¼ teaspoon salt
½ cup (1 stick) unsalted butter, room temperature
¼ cup firmly packed light brown sugar
1 cup orange marmalade
2 eggs
Whipped cream (optional)

For topping: Generously butter 9-inch cake pan with 3-inch sides. Stir first 4 ingredients in heavy medium saucepan over low heat until sugar dissolves. Spread evenly in prepared pan. Cool 5 minutes. Top with berries.

For cake: Position rack in center of oven and preheat to 350°F. Sift first 5 ingredients into bowl. Using electric mixer, cream butter in another bowl. Add sugar and beat until light and fluffy. Beat in marmalade. Blend in half of flour mixture. Mix in eggs. Blend in remaining flour. Spoon batter atop cranberries. Bake until cake is firm to touch, about 70 minutes.

Cool cake in pan on rack 10 minutes. Run knife around cake. Invert onto platter. Serve warm or at room temperature. Pass cream if desired.

Currant-Lemon Cake

For best flavor, make this delicate cake the day before you serve it.

8 to 10 servings

Butter
All purpose flour
14 tablespoons (1¾ sticks) butter, room temperature
¾ cup sugar
3 eggs, room temperature

1½ cups unbleached all purpose flour
1½ cups dried currants
2½ teaspoons finely grated lemon peel
2 teaspoons cinnamon
½ teaspoon baking soda
¼ cup fresh lemon juice

Position rack in lower third of oven and preheat to 350°F. Butter and flour 7-cup tube pan or bundt pan. Using electric mixer, cream 14 tablespoons butter and sugar until light. Add eggs 1 at a time and beat until light and fluffy. Thoroughly combine 1½ cups flour, currants, lemon peel, cinnamon and baking soda; add to batter with lemon juice. Mix just until well combined. Spread batter evenly in prepared pan. Bake until tester inserted in center comes out clean, 45 to 50 minutes. Cool cake in pan on rack 20 minutes. Invert onto rack and cool completely. Wrap tightly with foil and let flavors mellow overnight.

Ginger-Lemon Marble Cake

Makes one 8x4-inch loaf

Light Batter
½ cup (1 stick) butter, room temperature
¾ cup sugar
2 eggs, room temperature
1 tablespoon grated lemon peel
¾ cup all purpose flour
½ teaspoon baking powder
Pinch of salt
¼ cup milk

Dark Batter
¼ cup (½ stick) butter, room temperature

¼ cup firmly packed light brown sugar
1 egg, room temperature
½ cup molasses
⅔ cup all purpose flour
1 teaspoon cinnamon
1 teaspoon ground ginger
½ teaspoon freshly grated nutmeg
¼ teaspoon ground cloves
¼ teaspoon ground cardamom
¼ teaspoon baking soda
3 tablespoons finely chopped candied ginger

Preheat oven to 325°F. Butter and lightly flour 8x4-inch loaf pan.

For light batter: Cream butter in medium bowl of electric mixer until fluffy. Gradually beat in sugar. Beat in eggs one at a time. Blend in lemon peel. Sift in dry ingredients alternately with milk, stirring gently with spoon until just blended; be careful to not overmix.

For dark batter: Cream butter in medium bowl of electric mixer until fluffy. Beat in brown sugar and egg. Blend in molasses until smooth and slightly lightened in color. Sift in flour, spices and soda, stirring gently with wooden spoon until just blended. Fold candied ginger into batter.

Drop alternating spoonfuls of light and dark batter into prepared pan. Swirl through with knife several times in each direction to marbleize. Bake until tester inserted in center comes out clean, about 1½ hours. Cool cake completely in pan on rack before serving.

Pear Kuchen

This easy, cardamom-scented cake has a crunchy almond topping.

10 servings

Almond Topping
- ¾ cup firmly packed dark brown sugar
- 1 tablespoon bleached all purpose flour
- ½ teaspoon freshly ground cardamom
- 2 tablespoons (¼ stick) well-chilled unsalted butter
- 1 cup chopped toasted unblanched almonds

Cardamom Cake
- 2 cups sifted bleached all purpose flour
- 1 teaspoon baking powder
- 1 teaspoon baking soda
- 1 teaspoon freshly ground cardamom
- ¼ scant teaspoon salt
- ½ cup (1 stick) unsalted butter, room temperature
- 1 cup sugar
- 3 eggs, room temperature
- 1 teaspoon grated lemon peel
- 1 cup sour cream, room temperature
- ¾ pound pears, peeled, cored and cut into ⅓- to ½-inch dice

For topping: Blend sugar, flour and cardamom in medium bowl. Cut in butter until coarse meal forms. Mix in chopped almonds. Set aside.

For cake: Position rack in center of oven and preheat to 325°F. Grease 9x13-inch ovenproof glass baking dish. Sift first 5 ingredients into bowl. Using electric mixer, cream butter in another bowl. Add sugar and beat until light and fluffy. Beat in eggs 1 at a time. Mix in lemon peel. Blend in dry ingredients alternately with sour cream, beginning and ending with dry ingredients. Smooth batter in prepared dish. Top with pears. Sprinkle with topping. Bake until tester inserted in center comes out clean, about 40 minutes. Cool 25 minutes. Serve warm or at room temperature.

Upside-down Maple Sugar Pear Cake

Caramelized pears top a maple-scented cake. The maple sugar can be found at natural foods stores.

8 servings

Topping
- Unsalted butter, room temperature
- Granulated maple sugar
- 5 tablespoons unsalted butter, room temperature
- ⅓ cup firmly packed light brown sugar
- ¼ cup sugar
- 1 tablespoon pure maple syrup
- Pinch of salt
- 4 medium Comice pears, peeled, cored and cut lengthwise into 6 slices each

Cake
- 2 cups all purpose flour
- 1 teaspoon baking soda
- 1 teaspoon salt
- ¾ teaspoon cinnamon
- 1 cup granulated maple sugar
- 6 tablespoons (¾ stick) unsalted butter, room temperature
- 2 eggs, room temperature
- 1 cup sour cream
- ⅓ cup pure maple syrup
- ¾ cup English walnuts, toasted and finely chopped

Bourbon Whipped Cream*

For topping: Position rack in center of oven and preheat to 375°F. Generously butter bottom and sides of 9-inch-diameter 3-inch-deep cake pan. Sprinkle with maple sugar. Cream 5 tablespoons butter, brown sugar and sugar until light. Mix in maple syrup and salt. Spread evenly in prepared pan. Pat pear slices dry. Press into sugar mixture, arranging close together in spoke design.

For cake: Whisk together flour, soda, salt and cinnamon. Using electric mixer, cream maple sugar and butter until light and fluffy. Add eggs 1 at a time, beating until light. Add sour cream and beat until smooth. Mix in maple syrup. Fold in flour mixture, then walnuts. Pour batter into pear-lined pan. Bake until tester inserted in center comes out clean, 50 to 60 minutes. Let cool 12 minutes.

Run knife around edge of cake. Invert cake onto platter; leave pan atop cake 5 minutes. Gently remove pan. Cool cake 15 to 20 minutes. Serve warm, passing whipped cream separately.

*Bourbon Whipped Cream

Makes about 3 cups

1½ cups well-chilled whipping cream
  3 tablespoons powdered sugar

2 tablespoons bourbon

Beat cream until soft peaks form. Add sugar and bourbon and continue beating until soft peaks form again.

Edna Lou's Sour Cream Cake

Makes one 9x5-inch loaf

½ cup ground toasted walnuts
⅓ cup firmly packed brown sugar
 1 ounce finely grated unsweetened chocolate

½ cup (1 stick) butter, room temperature
 1 cup sugar

2 eggs, room temperature
2 teaspoons vanilla
2 cups all purpose flour
2 teaspoons baking powder
1 teaspoon baking soda
1 cup sour cream, room temperature

Preheat oven to 325°F. Combine walnuts, brown sugar and grated chocolate in small bowl. Set mixture aside.

Butter and flour 9x5-inch loaf pan. Cream ½ cup butter in large bowl of electric mixer until fluffy. Gradually beat in sugar. Beat in eggs one at a time. Blend in vanilla. Sift flour with baking powder and soda. Using wooden spoon, stir dry ingredients into batter alternately with sour cream.

Spread ⅓ of batter in prepared pan. Sprinkle evenly with ⅓ of nut mixture. Repeat layering 2 more times, ending with nut mixture. Bake until tester inserted in center comes out clean, about 1 hour. Cool in pan.

Chocolate and Almond Tea Cake

This is best served the same day it is made.

8 to 10 servings

½ large orange
⅓ cup sugar
 1 cup cake flour
 1 teaspoon baking powder
½ teaspoon ground cardamom
¾ cup (4 ounces) blanched almonds, toasted and finely ground
¾ cup semisweet chocolate chips
1½ teaspoons light rum
1½ tablespoons all purpose flour

½ cup (1 stick) butter
½ cup firmly packed light brown sugar
 1 egg yolk
 1 teaspoon vanilla
¾ teaspoon almond extract
 3 eggs
 2 tablespoons whipping cream
 1 cup (4 ounces) sliced almonds
 3 tablespoons powdered sugar

Position rack in center of oven and preheat to 325°F. Grease and flour 10-inch spring-form pan. Remove orange peel (orange part only) using vegetable peeler. Finely grind peel with sugar in processor. Sift together cake flour, baking powder and cardamom. Mix in ground almonds. Combine chocolate chips and rum. Sprinkle with all purpose flour and stir to coat chips completely. Beat butter in large bowl of electric mixer until light and fluffy. Add orange peel mixture and brown sugar and beat well. Blend in yolk, vanilla and almond extract. Beat in eggs 1 at a time. Gently beat flour-almond mixture and cream alternately into butter mixture, stopping to scrape down sides of bowl. Fold in chocolate chips. Turn batter into prepared pan, smoothing top. Sprinkle with sliced almonds. Dust with powdered sugar. Bake until tester inserted in center comes out clean, about 55 minutes. Cool in pan on rack 5 minutes. Carefully remove springform. Serve cake warm or at room temperature.

Chocolate-Banana Cake

8 servings

Unsweetened cocoa powder
1¼ cups sifted bleached all purpose flour
½ cup unsweetened cocoa powder
1 teaspoon baking powder
½ teaspoon baking soda
¼ teaspoon salt
½ cup (1 stick) unsalted butter, room temperature

1 cup firmly packed dark brown sugar
1 teaspoon instant coffee powder
2 eggs, room temperature
1 tablespoon grated orange peel
1 cup banana puree (from about 3 large very ripe bananas)
1 cup semisweet chocolate chips
Powdered sugar

Position rack in center of oven and preheat to 325°F. Butter 6-cup fluted tube pan; dust with cocoa powder. Sift next 5 ingredients into bowl. Using electric mixer, cream butter in another bowl. Add brown sugar and coffee powder and beat until light and fluffy. Beat in eggs 1 at a time, then beat 2 minutes. Add orange peel. Mix in dry ingredients alternately with banana puree, beginning and ending with dry ingredients. Fold in chocolate chips. Spoon batter into prepared pan. Bake until cake is firm to touch in center, about 70 minutes. Cool in pan 10 minutes. Invert onto rack and cool completely. Dust cake with powdered sugar just before serving.

Chocolate, Prune and Cognac Cake

12 servings

¾ pound soft-pack pitted prunes, cut into raisin-size pieces
⅓ cup Cognac or brandy
3 tablespoons sugar

9 ounces semisweet chocolate, coarsely chopped
5 tablespoons Cognac or brandy
2 teaspoons instant coffee powder
14 tablespoons (1¾ sticks) unsalted butter, cut into tablespoons
¾ cup sugar
14 tablespoons unbleached all purpose flour

1 teaspoon cinnamon
¾ teaspoon ground allspice
5 eggs, separated, room temperature

Pinch of salt
Pinch of cream of tartar
¼ cup sugar

Chocolate Glaze
6 tablespoons whipping cream
4½ ounces semisweet chocolate, finely chopped
3 tablespoons Cognac or brandy

Combine prunes, ⅓ cup Cognac and 3 tablespoons sugar in heavy small saucepan. Bring to simmer, stirring constantly. Remove from heat. Cover and let steep 2 hours.

Melt chocolate with 5 tablespoons Cognac and coffee powder in heavy 2-quart saucepan over low heat, stirring constantly. Whisk in butter 1 tablespoon at a time. Mix in ¾ cup sugar, flour, cinnamon and allspice. Blend in yolks. Cool mixture slightly.

Preheat oven to 350°F. Butter 8- to 10-cup kugelhopf or bundt pan; dust with flour. Using electric mixer, beat whites, salt and cream of tartar until soft peaks form. Add ¼ cup sugar 1 tablespoon at a time and beat until almost stiff but not dry. Whisk chocolate mixture to loosen. Gently fold in ¼ of whites. Fold mixture back into remaining whites. Gently fold in prunes. Pour batter into prepared pan. Bake until center is firm to touch and a few crumbs stick to tester inserted into center, about 1 hour. Cool in pan 25 minutes. Invert onto rack and cool completely. Wrap tightly and let stand at room temperature overnight.

For glaze: Bring cream to simmer in heavy small saucepan. Remove from heat. Stir in chocolate. Cover and let stand 5 minutes. Add Cognac. Cool until glaze mounds slightly on spoon.

Spoon glaze over cake, allowing to drip down sides. Let stand until glaze is set.

Pound Cakes

Old World Sour Cream Pound Cake

8 to 10 servings

1 cup (2 sticks) butter, room temperature
2¾ cups sugar
6 eggs, room temperature
3 cups sifted all purpose flour

½ teaspoon salt
¼ teaspoon baking soda
1¼ cups sour cream
1 teaspoon vanilla

Preheat oven to 350°F. Grease and flour 10-inch tube pan. Cream butter with sugar using electric mixer. Add eggs one at a time, beating well after each addition. Sift flour with salt and baking soda. Add flour to butter mixture in three batches alternately with sour cream, mixing well after each addition. Blend in vanilla. Pour batter into prepared pan. Bake until top is light brown and tester inserted near center comes out clean, about 1¼ hours. Cool cake completely in pan before serving.

Scandinavian Pound Cake

Potato flour or cornstarch gives the "sand" texture to this buttery cake.

16 to 20 servings

2 tablespoons (¼ stick) butter, room temperature
¼ cup pearl sugar or coarsely crushed sugar cubes
1 cup (2 sticks) unsalted butter, room temperature
1 cup sugar
4 eggs, room temperature

2 tablespoons brandy
1 teaspoon vanilla
2 cups all purpose flour
¼ cup cornstarch or potato flour
1 teaspoon baking powder
¼ teaspoon salt
¼ cup whipping cream

Preheat oven to 325°F. Grease 6-cup kugelhopf pan or other decorative bundt pan with 2 tablespoons butter. Sprinkle with pearl sugar. Cream 1 cup butter with 1 cup sugar in large bowl of electric mixer. Beat in eggs until light. Mix in brandy and vanilla. Thoroughly combine flour, cornstarch, baking powder and salt in small bowl. Beat into butter mixture with cream just until batter is smooth.

Spread batter evenly in prepared pan. Bake until tester inserted in center comes out clean, about 50 minutes. Cool 5 minutes. Invert onto rack and cool completely. Wrap tightly with plastic. Let stand overnight at room temperature before serving.

Aunt Agnes's Apple Pound Cake

8 servings

2 pounds Granny Smith apples, peeled, cored and thinly sliced	4 eggs
5 tablespoons sugar	¼ cup fresh orange juice
2 tablespoons cinnamon	1 tablespoon baking powder
3 cups all purpose flour	2½ teaspoons vanilla
2½ cups sugar	½ teaspoon salt
1 cup vegetable oil	
	Powdered sugar

Preheat oven to 350°F. Grease 10-inch tube pan. Combine apples, 5 tablespoons sugar and cinnamon; set aside. In large bowl of electric mixer, combine flour, sugar, oil, eggs, juice, baking powder, vanilla and salt. Beat until thoroughly incorporated (batter will be heavy). Spoon half of batter into prepared pan. Top with half of apples. Repeat with remaining batter and apples. Bake until top of pound cake is brown and firm to touch, about 1¾ hours.

Cool cake 1½ hours. Remove from pan. Sprinkle lightly with powdered sugar. Serve pound cake warm.

Coconut Pound Cake with Lemon Curd Filling

Beautiful, rich and sweet, but balanced by the tart lemon curd. A wonderful do-ahead party dessert.

12 servings

Solid vegetable shortening	2 teaspoons vanilla
All purpose flour	
1½ cups (3 sticks) unsalted butter, room temperature	Lemon Curd Filling*
3 cups sugar	*Orange Glaze*
6 eggs, room temperature	1 cup fresh orange juice
3 cups all purpose flour	¾ cup sugar
¼ teaspoon salt	2 tablespoons fresh lemon juice
¼ teaspoon baking soda	1 teaspoon almond extract
1 cup sour cream	
4 ounces flaked coconut	Lemon leaves

Preheat oven to 300°F. Generously grease 10-inch tube pan (preferably with removable bottom) with vegetable shortening and dust with flour. Cream butter in large bowl of electric mixer. Slowly add sugar, beating until light and fluffy. Beat in eggs 1 at a time. Sift dry ingredients. Blend into butter mixture alternately with sour cream. Mix in coconut and vanilla. Spoon batter into prepared pan. Bake until tester inserted in center comes out clean, about 1½ hours. Cool cake in pan on rack 30 minutes. Invert cake onto rack and cool completely.

Cut cake in half to make 2 layers, using serrated knife. Fill with 1¼ cups lemon curd; spread ¼ cup on top.

For glaze: Heat all ingredients in heavy small saucepan over low heat, swirling pan occasionally, until sugar dissolves. Increase heat and boil until mixture is reduced by ¼, about 5 minutes.

Immediately pour glaze over top of cake, allowing some to drizzle down sides. *(Cake can be prepared 1 day ahead. Cover and store at room temperature.)* Surround cake with leaves. Pass remaining lemon curd separately.

*Lemon Curd Filling

This old-fashioned custard is also superb on scones or with fresh fruit.

Makes about 3½ cups

6 large lemons	6 eggs, room temperature, beaten
2 cups sugar	to blend
¾ cup (1½ sticks) unsalted butter, cut into 12 pieces	

Remove peel from lemons (yellow part only), using vegetable peeler. Chop finely in processor. Squeeze lemons and measure 1 cup juice. Heat juice with peel, sugar and butter in double boiler over simmering water until sugar dissolves and butter melts. Strain eggs into lemon mixture. Cook until custard leaves path on back of spoon when finger is drawn across, stirring constantly, about 20 minutes; *do not boil.* Pour into jar or bowl. Place plastic wrap on surface to prevent skin from forming; let cool. Cover and refrigerate overnight before using. *(Can be refrigerated up to 1 month.)*

Chocolate Chip and Currant Pound Cake

This distinctive treat can be baked in either a loaf pan or fluted tube cake pan.

8 to 10 servings

¾ cup dried currants	2 tablespoons bleached all purpose flour
3 tablespoons Armagnac or Cognac	¾ cup (1½ sticks) unsalted butter, room temperature
1½ cups bleached all purpose flour	1 cup sugar
1½ teaspoons baking powder	3 eggs, room temperature
½ teaspoon cinnamon	
⅜ teaspoon salt	Powdered sugar
6 tablespoons half and half	Armagnac Glaze* (optional)
1 teaspoon vanilla	Semisweet chocolate curls
5 ounces extra-bittersweet (not unsweetened) or semisweet chocolate, cut into ¼-inch pieces	Sugared grapes (optional)

Heat currants and Armagnac in small saucepan until just warm. Cover mixture and let stand 1 hour.

Position rack in center of oven and preheat to 350°F. Butter 6-cup fluted tube cake pan or 9x5-inch loaf pan. (Line loaf pan with waxed paper; butter paper.) Dust pan with flour. Sift 1½ cups flour, baking powder, cinnamon and salt into medium bowl. Drain soaking liquid from currants into half and half. Add vanilla. Pat currants dry. Combine currants, bittersweet chocolate and 2 tablespoons flour in small bowl. Using electric mixer, cream butter in large bowl. Add 1 cup sugar and beat until light and fluffy. Beat in eggs 1 at a time. Mix flour and half and half mixtures alternately into butter, beginning and ending with flour mixture. Using spatula, fold in chocolate mixture. Spoon into prepared pan. Bake cake until center is springy to touch, about 1 hour.

Cool cake in pan on rack 15 minutes. Run knife around cake. Invert onto rack. Peel off paper and cool cake completely. Sprinkle with powdered sugar or spread glaze over top, allowing some to drip down sides. Garnish with chocolate curls and grapes.

*Armagnac Glaze

Makes about ½ cup

¾ cup powdered sugar, sifted
1½ tablespoons unsalted butter, room temperature

1 tablespoon (or more) Armagnac or Cognac
1 teaspoon whipping cream

Blend sugar, butter, cream and Armagnac in processor until fluffy.

French Lemon Loaf Cake

8 to 10 servings

1½ cups cake flour
1 teaspoon baking powder
⅛ teaspoon salt
¾ cup plus 2 tablespoons sugar
2 tablespoons grated lemon peel
3 eggs

¾ cup (1½ sticks) unsalted butter, cut into 6 pieces, room temperature

½ cup powdered sugar
3 tablespoons fresh lemon juice

Position rack in center of oven and preheat to 325°F. Generously butter 6-cup loaf pan. Set aside.

Mix flour, baking powder and salt in processor 3 seconds. Set aside. Process ¾ cup plus 2 tablespoons sugar and lemon peel until peel is very finely minced. Add eggs and blend 1 minute, stopping once to scrape down sides of work bowl. Add butter and blend 1 minute. Spoon reserved dry ingredients around inside of work bowl and mix using 2 on/off turns. Run spatula around inside of work bowl to loosen mixture. Blend until ingredients are just combined, using 1 or 2 on/off turns. Transfer batter to prepared pan. Bake until tester inserted in center comes out clean, about 55 minutes. Cool in pan 5 minutes. Invert onto rack, then turn right side up.

Mix powdered sugar and lemon juice in small bowl. Brush on top and sides of hot cake. Cool completely. *(Can be prepared 3 days ahead. Wrap tightly and store at room temperature.)*

Lemon-Aniseed Pound Cake

Makes one 4½x12-inch loaf

¾ cup (1½ sticks) unsalted butter, room temperature
2½ cups sugar
3 eggs, separated, room temperature
5 teaspoons finely grated lemon peel
1½ teaspoons aniseed
1 teaspoon vanilla

2¼ cups all purpose flour
2 teaspoons baking powder
½ teaspoon salt
¾ cup milk, room temperature
Pinch of salt
Pinch of cream of tartar
1 tablespoon instant espresso powder

Position rack in center of oven and preheat to 350°F. Grease and flour 4½x12-inch loaf pan. Using electric mixer, cream butter and sugar in large bowl until light and fluffy. Beat in yolks 1 at a time. Blend in peel, aniseed and vanilla. Sift together flour, baking powder and ½ teaspoon salt. Mix into batter alternately with milk. Using electric mixer with clean dry beaters, beat whites with pinch of salt and cream of tartar in large bowl until stiff but not dry. Fold half of whites into batter to loosen. Fold in remaining whites. Spoon half of batter into prepared pan. Sprinkle evenly with espresso powder. Spoon in remaining batter. Bake until golden brown and tester inserted in center comes out clean, about 1½ hours. Cool 20 minutes in pan. Invert onto rack and cool completely. Chill overnight. Bring cake to room temperature before slicing.

Orange and Lemon Sour Cream Cake

12 servings

Cake

2 cups all purpose flour
1 teaspoon baking powder
1 teaspoon baking soda
1 cup (2 sticks) butter, room temperature
1 cup sugar
4 eggs, separated, room temperature
1 cup sour cream, room temperature
1 tablespoon minced orange peel
1 tablespoon minced lemon peel
Pinch of cream of tartar

Syrup

¾ cup sugar
¼ cup orange liqueur
¼ cup fresh orange juice
3 tablespoons fresh lemon juice
¼ teaspoon salt

6 thin lemon slices
6 orange slices
1 cup whipping cream, whipped

For cake: Preheat oven to 325°F. Butter and flour 9-inch tube cake pan. Sift together flour, baking powder and baking soda. Using electric mixer, cream butter and sugar. Add yolks, sour cream and orange and lemon peels and beat until slowly dissolving ribbon forms when beaters are lifted. Stir in dry ingredients. Using clean dry beaters, beat whites with cream of tartar until stiff but not dry. Gently fold half of whites into batter to lighten, then fold in remaining whites. Pour into prepared pan. Bake until tester inserted in center comes out clean, about 1 hour. Let cool in pan 15 minutes. Run knife around cake to loosen; invert onto platter.

For syrup: Cook all ingredients in heavy small saucepan over low heat until sugar dissolves, swirling pan. Increase heat and boil until syrupy.

Pierce top of cake. Pour syrup over. Garnish with lemon and orange slices. Serve with whipped cream.

English Chestnut Pound Cake

10 to 12 servings

2½ cups all purpose flour
1 cup sugar
2 teaspoons baking soda
3 eggs, room temperature
½ cup corn oil
1 17½-ounce can chestnut spread*
½ teaspoon almond extract

½ cup brandy
Powdered sugar
Fresh strawberries (optional)
Whipped cream
Chestnuts in brandy syrup,*
drained and coarsely crumbled

Preheat oven to 350°F. Generously grease 8-inch-diameter springform pan. Combine flour, sugar and baking soda in large bowl. Add eggs, oil, chestnut spread and almond extract and beat until well blended. Spread batter in prepared pan, smoothing top. Bake until tester inserted in center comes out clean, about 1½ hours. Cool 30 minutes in pan on rack.

Remove pan sides. Invert cake onto plate; remove pan bottom. Spoon half of brandy over cake. Invert cake onto platter. Spoon remaining brandy over top. Cool completely. *(Can be prepared 1 day ahead. Wrap tightly.)* Just before serving, dust cake with powdered sugar. Garnish with berries. Top cake slices with whipped cream and brandied chestnuts.

*Available in specialty foods stores, Italian markets and some supermarkets.

Raspberry and Blueberry Pound Cake

10 to 12 servings

5 eggs
1⅔ cups sugar
1¼ cups (2½ sticks) unsalted butter, cut into tablespoon-size pieces, room temperature
2 tablespoons kirsch
2 cups plus 8 tablespoons cake flour

1 teaspoon baking powder
½ teaspoon salt

1 cup fresh raspberries
1 cup fresh blueberries
Ice cream

Generously butter 9-cup bundt pan. Dust with flour, shaking out excess.

Blend eggs and sugar in processor until smooth and thick, about 1 minute, stopping once to scrape down sides of work bowl. Add butter pieces and kirsch and blend until fluffy, about 1 minute, stopping once to scrape down sides of work bowl. Add 2 cups plus 6 tablespoons flour, baking powder and salt and blend into butter mixture using 2 on/off turns.

Toss remaining 2 tablespoons flour with raspberries and blueberries in large bowl. Fold batter into berry mixture using rubber spatula. Transfer mixture to prepared pan, spreading evenly. Place pan on center rack in cold oven. Turn oven to 300°F. Bake until tester inserted in center comes out clean, about 1 hour 25 minutes. Cool in pan 5 minutes. Invert onto rack and cool completely. *(Can be prepared 1 day ahead, wrapped tightly and refrigerated.)* Serve at room temperature with ice cream.

2 ❧ Classic Frosted, Filled and Layer Cakes

A tall white layer cake filled and iced with fluffy marshmallow frosting and sprinkled with shredded coconut...a pretty, lavender-tinted jam cake, heady with spices and covered with a rich, sweet jam-and-raisin glaze...spongy cake roll filled with sweet cream and bright-colored fruit preserves. These are the kinds of classic desserts we think of when we think "cake."

And this chapter has plenty of such favorites, from delicate Angel Food Cake with Strawberries and Brown Sugar Sauce (page 28) and Rich Chocolate Layer Cake (page 40), moist and extra chocolatey, with a cloak of creamy, coffee-scented frosting, to Fresh Strawberry Cake Roll (page 47), topped and filled with berries and whipped cream—impressive but prepared in three easy steps. (In fact, many of these recipes are surprisingly quick and easy to do, particularly with the help of the food processor.)

You will find our variations on a classic theme far from ordinary. Try the rich Rum Fudge Cake with White Chocolate Glaze (page 30) and festive Tea Cake with Lemon Custard Icing and Fresh Berries (page 35). Swedish Laggtarta (page 38) is an unusual creation of thin layers of sponge cake. Each is baked in a heavy skillet, filled with an applesauce-strawberry mixture and stacked high on the serving platter. Cut it into wedges and garnish with whipped cream and marinated berries. For people who have not outgrown their love for the old-fashioned jelly roll, we have plenty of ideas, from a refreshingly tart Lemon-Lime Roll (page 46) to a gorgeous Praline and Pear Cake Roll (page 48), filled and frosted with crunchy almond praline buttercream.

❧ Single Layer and Tube Cakes

Angel Food Cake with Strawberries and Brown Sugar Sauce

A terrific old-fashioned cake.

10 servings

Cake
- 1 cup sifted cake flour
- 1¼ cups superfine sugar
- 1½ cups egg whites (about 12), room temperature
- 2 tablespoons fresh lemon juice
- 1½ teaspoons cream of tartar
- 1 teaspoon vanilla
- ½ teaspoon salt
- ¼ teaspoon lemon extract

Brown Sugar Sauce
- 2 cups sour cream
- ½ cup firmly packed light brown sugar

- 4 pints strawberries, thickly sliced
- ½ cup (about) sugar

For cake: Position rack in center of oven and preheat to 350°F. Resift flour with ½ cup sugar 3 times. Using electric mixer, beat whites in large bowl until foamy. Add lemon juice, cream of tartar, vanilla, salt and lemon extract and beat until soft peaks form. Add remaining ¾ cup sugar 2 tablespoons at a time, beating until stiff and glossy. Sift ⅓ of flour over whites. Gently but quickly fold in, using rubber spatula. Repeat, adding remaining flour in 2 batches and folding until just combined. Spoon batter into ungreased 10-inch tube pan. Run knife through batter several times to break up any bubbles. Bake until cake springs back when pressed in center, 40 to 45 minutes. Invert pan on rack and let cake cool completely in pan.

    For sauce: Whisk sour cream in medium bowl until smooth and shiny. Whisk in brown sugar. Cover and refrigerate until ready to serve.

    Combine strawberries with sugar to taste. Let stand until juices exude, stirring occasionally, about 30 minutes.

    Gently pull cake from sides of pan, using fork. Set on platter. To serve, cut into 1-inch slices, using 2 forks or angel cake cutter. Place slice on each plate. Top with sliced strawberries and sauce.

Apple Raisin Spice Cake with Pecan Vanilla Ice Cream and Caramel Sauce

Store-bought pecan or vanilla ice cream can be served with this scrumptious dessert.

8 to 10 servings

Cake
- 2 cups all purpose flour
- 1 cup cake flour
- 1½ teaspoons baking soda
- ½ teaspoon freshly grated nutmeg
- ½ teaspoon cinnamon
- ½ teaspoon salt
- ¼ teaspoon ground cloves
- ¼ teaspoon ground mace
- ¼ teaspoon ground ginger
- 1½ cups (3 sticks) butter, room temperature
- 2 cups sugar
- 3 eggs
- 3½ cups chopped, unpeeled tart green apples

- 1 cup raisins, soaked overnight in ½ cup bourbon and drained
- ¾ cup chopped roasted pecans

Sauce
- 1 cup whipping cream
- 1 cup firmly packed light brown sugar
- ⅓ cup sugar
- ¼ cup maple syrup
- ¼ cup dark corn syrup

    Pecan Vanilla Ice Cream*
    Crème fraîche or whipping cream

For cake: Preheat oven to 325°F. Butter and flour 10-inch springform pan. Sift together first 9 ingredients. Using electric mixer, cream butter and sugar until light and fluffy. Beat in eggs 1 at a time. Gradually fold in dry ingredients. Fold in apples, raisins and pecans. Spread batter in prepared pan. Bake until tester inserted in center comes out clean, about 1¾ hours. Cool cake completely.

For sauce: Cook first 5 ingredients in heavy deep 2-quart saucepan over high heat until mixture thickens and candy thermometer registers 220°F. Let sauce cool for 20 minutes, skimming foam from surface if necessary.

To serve, slice cake. Set on plates. Top with ice cream. Spoon sauce onto plates; drizzle crème fraîche over sauce.

*Pecan Vanilla Ice Cream

Makes 2 quarts

4 cups milk
2 cups chopped roasted pecans
2 vanilla beans, split

12 egg yolks

1⅓ cups sugar
1½ cups well-chilled whipping cream
or crème fraîche

Combine milk, pecans and vanilla beans in heavy large saucepan and bring to boil. Remove from heat. Cover and let stand 15 minutes.

Whisk yolks and sugar in large bowl until thick and pale. Return milk to boil. Slowly strain milk into bowl, whisking constantly. Return milk mixture to saucepan. Set pan over low heat and cook until custard thickens and candy thermometer registers 185°F, stirring constantly with wooden spoon; do not boil.

Immediately set saucepan in large ice-filled bowl. Stir in cream. Let stand until custard is thoroughly chilled.

Transfer custard to ice cream maker and processs according to manufacturer's instructions. Freeze several hours to mellow. Soften ice cream slightly in refrigerator before serving, if necessary.

Southern Blackberry Jam Cake

A delicately spiced, walnut-studded cake with a fragrant hint of orange.

10 servings

2⅓ cups all purpose flour
⅓ cup finely ground walnuts
2 teaspoons baking soda
1 teaspoon cinnamon
1 teaspoon ground allspice
1 teaspoon freshly grated nutmeg
1 teaspoon salt
¾ cup (1½ sticks) butter, room temperature
1 cup sugar
3 eggs, room temperature

¾ cup strained blackberry or black raspberry jam
3 tablespoons bourbon
2 teaspoons finely grated orange peel
¾ cup buttermilk
1 cup finely chopped toasted walnuts

½ cup strained blackberry or black raspberry jam
Powdered sugar
Whipped cream

Position rack in lower third of oven and preheat to 350°F. Generously grease 10-cup fluted tube pan or kugelhupf mold; dust with sugar. Whisk flour, ⅓ cup ground walnuts, baking soda, cinnamon, allspice, nutmeg and salt in medium bowl to blend. Using electric mixer, cream butter and 1 cup sugar until light and fluffy. Add eggs 1 at a time, beating until very light. Mix in ¾ cup jam, then bourbon and orange peel. Blend in dry ingredients alternately with buttermilk, beginning and ending with dry ingredients. Fold in 1 cup walnuts.

Pour ⅓ of batter into prepared pan. Dot with ¼ cup jam. Pour in another ⅓ of batter and dot with remaining ¼ cup jam. Top with remaining batter. Insert small knife ⅔ of the way into pan and swirl through batter. Bake until cake is springy to touch and begins to pull away from sides of pan, about 55 minutes. Cool in pan on rack 20 minutes. Invert onto rack, remove pan and cool cake completely. *(Can be prepared 1 day ahead. Wrap tightly.)* Dust cake lightly with powdered sugar. Serve with whipped cream.

Eggless Chocolate Cake

8 to 10 servings

1½ cups all purpose flour
1 cup sugar
3 tablespoons unsweetened cocoa powder
1½ teaspoons baking powder
1 teaspoon baking soda
½ teaspoon salt
1 cup cold water
¼ cup plus 1 tablespoon corn oil
1 tablespoon distilled white vinegar
1 teaspoon vanilla
Cream Cheese Frosting* (optional)

Preheat oven to 350°F. Grease and flour 8-inch square cake pan and set aside. Sift flour, sugar, cocoa, baking powder, soda and salt into medium bowl. Make well in center. Add water, oil, vinegar and vanilla to well and beat until smooth, about 2 to 3 minutes (batter will be thin). Pour into prepared pan. Bake until tester inserted in center comes out clean, about 30 to 35 minutes. Invert cake onto wire rack and let cool. Frost top and sides of cake with Cream Cheese Frosting if desired. Cover and refrigerate before serving.

*Cream Cheese Frosting

Makes about 2½ cups

1 3-ounce package cream cheese, room temperature
¼ cup plus 2 tablespoons (¾ stick) butter, room temperature
½ teaspoon vanilla
2 cups powdered sugar

Beat cream cheese and butter in large mixing bowl until smooth. Add vanilla and blend with wooden spoon. Stir in sugar ⅓ cup at a time, beating thoroughly.

Rum Fudge Cake with White Chocolate Glaze

12 servings

Unsweetened cocoa powder
1½ cups plus 2 tablespoons cake flour
1½ teaspoons baking powder
¾ teaspoon baking soda
¾ teaspoon salt
4 ounces unsweetened chocolate, coarsely chopped
½ cup boiling water
3 tablespoons unsweetened cocoa powder
1 cup (2 sticks) unsalted butter, room temperature
1½ cups sugar
3 egg yolks
¾ cup whipping cream
2 tablespoons dark rum
5 egg whites
⅛ teaspoon cream of tartar
¼ cup sugar

White Chocolate Glaze*

Position rack in center of oven and preheat to 350°F. Generously butter 12-cup bundt pan; dust with cocoa powder. Sift flour, baking powder, baking soda and salt together.

Melt chocolate in top of double boiler over barely simmering water. Pour boiling water and 3 tablespoons cocoa powder into small bowl. Whisk in chocolate. Cool chocolate mixture slightly.

Using electric mixer, cream butter and 1½ cups sugar until light and fluffy. Add yolks and mix until fluffy, about 2 minutes. Using rubber spatula, fold in chocolate mixture, then cream and rum. Fold in dry ingredients. Beat whites and cream of tartar until mixture begins to hold shape. Add ¼ cup sugar 1 tablespoon at a time and beat until whites are glossy and hold soft peaks. Fold ¼ of whites into batter; gently fold in remaining whites. Pour into prepared pan. Bake until tester inserted in center comes out clean, about 55 minutes. Cool in pan on rack 10 minutes (cake will fall slightly). Invert onto rack and cool completely.

Place rack with cake over large baking sheet. Spoon glaze over top, allowing some to drip down sides. Serve cake at room temperature. (*Rum Fudge Cake can be prepared 1 day ahead. Wrap tightly.*)

*White Chocolate Glaze

Makes about 1 cup

4 ounces imported white chocolate, coarsely chopped
1 cup powdered sugar, sifted
¼ cup sour cream

4½ teaspoons dark rum
1 tablespoon unsalted butter, room temperature
Pinch of salt

Melt chocolate in top of double boiler over barely simmering water. Transfer to 2-quart bowl and cool slightly. Add sugar and stir until smooth. Mix in sour cream, rum, butter and salt.

Souffléed Chestnut Cake

This started out as a way to use leftover chestnut puree—the final result was a rich and refined dessert.

12 servings

Butter
½ cup (1 stick) unsalted butter, room temperature
⅔ cup sugar
1 tablespoon grated orange peel
3 egg yolks, room temperature
1½ cups canned unsweetened chestnut puree
3 ounces semisweet chocolate, melted and cooled slightly

3 tablespoons dark rum or orange liqueur
2½ tablespoons all purpose flour
1 teaspoon vanilla

4 egg whites, room temperature
Pinch of salt
2 tablespoons sugar
Powdered sugar
Whipped cream

Preheat oven to 375°F. Butter and flour 9-inch springform pan. Using electric mixer, beat ½ cup butter until light. Add ⅔ cup sugar and orange peel and beat until light and fluffy. Beat in yolks 1 at a time. Add chestnut puree, chocolate, rum, flour and vanilla and beat until smooth.

Using electric mixer with clean dry beaters, beat whites with salt until soft peaks form. Gradually add 2 tablespoons sugar and beat until stiff and shiny. Gently fold ¼ of whites into chestnut mixture. Fold in remaining whites. Pour batter into prepared pan. Bake until lightly puffed and barely set in center, 30 to 35 minutes. Cool slightly on wire rack. Carefully remove springform. (Cake will sink as it cools.) Place doily over cake and sprinkle with powdered sugar to create decorative pattern. Carefully remove doily. Serve cake with whipped cream.

 Layer Cakes

Blackberry Jam Cake

8 to 10 servings

Cake
- 1 cup (2 sticks) butter, room temperature
- 2 cups sugar
- 6 eggs, room temperature
- 1 cup buttermilk
- 4 cups sifted all purpose flour
- 1 teaspoon baking soda
- ½ teaspoon cinnamon
- ½ teaspoon ground cloves
- 1 cup seedless blackberry jam
- 1 cup chopped walnuts
- 1 teaspoon vanilla

Glaze
- 3 cups sugar
- 1 cup whipping cream
- ½ cup (1 stick) butter
- 1 cup seedless blackberry jam
- 1 cup raisins

For cake: Preheat oven to 350°F. Grease and flour four 8-inch round cake pans. Cream butter with sugar in large bowl of electric mixer. Add eggs 1 at a time, beating well after each addition. Mix in buttermilk. Combine flour, baking soda, cinnamon and cloves in another large bowl. Gradually add to butter mixture, beating until thoroughly incorporated. Stir in jam, nuts and vanilla. Pour batter into prepared pans. Bake until tester inserted in centers comes out clean, about 30 minutes. Cool on racks.

For glaze: Combine sugar, whipping cream and butter in heavy large saucepan over medium heat. Stir until syrup reaches 240°F on candy thermometer (soft-ball stage). Remove from heat and stir in jam and raisins. Cool 30 minutes.

To assemble: Even tops of cake layers with serrated knife. Transfer one layer to shallow-rimmed platter. Spoon some of glaze over top. Repeat with remaining layers and glaze, allowing glaze to drip down sides and form well around bottom of cake. Serve within 4 hours of assembly.

Chapman's Apple Cake

This cake is named after John Chapman, better known as Johnny Appleseed.

12 servings

Butter
- ½ cup (1 stick) unsalted butter, room temperature
- 2 cups sugar
- 2 teaspoons grated lemon peel
- 1 teaspoon cinnamon
- ½ teaspoon salt
- 2 eggs, room temperature
- ½ teaspoon baking soda
- ¾ cup milk
- 1¾ cups all purpose flour
- 1½ teaspoons baking powder
- 12 ounces pippin apples, peeled, cored and finely chopped

Spiced Apple Butter*
- 3 cups well-chilled whipping cream
- 2 tablespoons sugar
- 1 Red Delicious apple (optional), cored and thinly sliced
- Walnut halves (optional)

Preheat oven to 350°F. Butter two 8-inch-diameter cake pans. Line bottoms with parchment. Cream ½ cup butter in electric mixer. Add 2 cups sugar, lemon peel, cinnamon and salt and beat until light and fluffy. Add eggs 1 at a time, beating until smooth. Dissolve baking soda in milk; blend half into creamed mixture. Add half of flour and mix just until smooth. Mix in remaining milk, then baking powder and remaining flour, blending just until smooth. Using spoon, fold in chopped apples.

Divide batter between prepared pans. Bake until tester inserted in centers of cakes comes out clean, 35 to 40 minutes. Cool in pans on rack. *(Can be prepared 1 day ahead. Wrap tightly and refrigerate.)*

Just before serving, discard paper from cake layers. Trim sides to even if necessary. Place 1 layer on platter. Spread top with 1 cup apple butter. Top with second layer and spread with 1¼ cups apple butter (reserve remainder for another use). Beat cream to soft peaks. Add 2 tablespoons sugar and beat until firm peaks form. Spread some of cream over sides of cake. Spoon remainder into pastry bag fitted with star tip. Pipe rosettes of cream around top edge of cake. Garnish with apple slices and walnuts.

*Spiced Apple Butter

Makes about 3 cups

2 cups apple cider	½ teaspoon freshly grated nutmeg
¼ cup firmly packed light brown sugar	½ teaspoon ground cloves
½ teaspoon cinnamon	2½ pounds Rome Beauty apples, cored and quartered (do not peel)
½ teaspoon ground ginger	

Preheat oven to 350°F. Cook first 6 ingredients in heavy ovenproof Dutch oven over low heat, swirling pan occasionally, until sugar dissolves. Increase heat and bring to boil. Add apples and return to boil. Cover and bake until apples are very soft and liquid has evaporated, stirring occasionally, about 2 hours. Cool slightly. Puree in processor until smooth. *(Can be prepared 1 month ahead and chilled.)*

Pumpkin Maple Cake

8 to 10 servings

2 cups cake flour	¾ cup (1½ sticks) unsalted butter, room temperature, cut into 6 pieces
2 teaspoons baking powder	½ cup maple syrup
1½ teaspoons cinnamon	¾ cup solid pack pumpkin
½ teaspoon ground cloves	½ teaspoon maple flavoring
½ teaspoon baking soda	
¼ teaspoon salt	Pumpkin Cream Frosting*
3 eggs, separated, room temperature	15 pecan halves
2 teaspoons distilled white vinegar	
1½ cups sugar	

Position rack in center of oven and preheat to 350°F. Line 9-inch springform pan with parchment or waxed paper; butter pan and paper. Sift together flour, baking powder, cinnamon, cloves, baking soda and salt.

Blend whites 15 seconds in processor. With machine running, drizzle vinegar through feed tube and whip until whites hold shape, about 1½ minutes. Transfer to large bowl; do not clean work bowl. Add yolks and sugar to work bowl and blend 1 minute, stopping to scrape down sides of bowl. Add butter and mix 1 minute. With machine running, pour syrup through feed tube and mix 10 seconds. Add pumpkin and maple flavoring and blend 5 seconds. Spoon flour mixture in ring around inside of work bowl. Spoon whites onto mixture. Blend using 2 on/off turns. Run spatula around inside to loosen mixture. Using on/off turns, blend until ingredients are just combined; do not overmix. Spoon into prepared pan. Bake until tester inserted in center comes out clean, 50 to 60 minutes. Cool cake in pan 5 minutes. Remove from pan and cool completely.

Using long serrated knife, cut cake horizontally into 2 layers. Set top layer cut side up on platter. Spread with about ½ cup frosting. Cover with second cake layer cut side down. Spread top and sides with remaining frosting. Arange pecan halves around edge of cake. *(Can be prepared 2 days ahead. Cover and store at room temperature.)*

*Pumpkin Cream Frosting

Makes 1½ cups

1 8-ounce package cream cheese, room temperature, cut into 6 pieces
¾ cup powdered sugar

¼ cup solid pack pumpkin
1½ teaspoons vanilla

Mix all ingredients in processor until smooth, scraping down sides of work bowl. Cover and refrigerate until spreadable, about 10 minutes.

Maple Walnut Cake

10 to 12 servings

Cake
½ cup (1 stick) unsalted butter, room temperature
½ cup firmly packed light brown sugar
2 eggs, beaten to blend, room temperature
2½ cups cake flour
2 teaspoons baking powder
½ teaspoon baking soda
1 cup maple syrup
½ cup hot water

Maple Walnut Praline
1 cup maple syrup
1 cup chopped walnuts

Maple Whipped Cream
2 cups whipping cream
6 tablespoons powdered sugar
1 to 2 teaspoons maple extract

For cake: Preheat oven to 350°F. Grease two 8- or 9-inch round cake pans. Using electric mixer, cream butter and brown sugar. Beat in eggs in thin stream. Combine flour, baking powder and baking soda in another bowl. Alternate adding dry ingredients, syrup and hot water to butter mixture, blending until smooth. Pour batter into prepared pans. Bake until tester inserted in center comes out clean, about 30 minutes. Cool completely. Wrap; chill thoroughly.

For praline: Lightly grease baking sheet. Boil syrup in heavy small saucepan until candy thermometer registers 300°F (hard-crack stage). Remove from heat. Stir in walnuts. Pour onto prepared baking sheet. Cool until set. Transfer praline to processor and mix to fine powder.

For whipped cream: Beat cream with sugar and extract to stiff peaks.

To assemble: Cut off top crusts from cake layers. Set 1 layer on platter. Spread lightly with whipped cream. Sprinkle lightly with praline. Top with second cake layer. Spread top and sides lightly with whipped cream. Spoon remaining whipped cream into pastry bag fitted with star tip. Pipe lattice design atop cake; pipe border around bottom edge of cake. Press praline onto sides; sprinkle any remainder on top. Serve Maple Walnut Cake chilled or at room temperature.

Etruscan Rum Cake

12 servings

Cake
7 eggs
14 tablespoons sugar
1½ cups all purpose flour

Syrup
¼ cup sugar
¼ cup water
¼ cup light rum

Cream
3 cups whipping cream
½ cup sugar
4 ounces semisweet chocolate, melted

⅔ cup chopped husked hazelnuts
⅔ cup chopped blanched almonds
½ cup semisweet chocolate chips

Garnish
½ cup apricot jam, melted and sieved (glaze)
⅔ cup sliced almonds, toasted
½ cup chopped husked hazelnuts
¼ cup semisweet chocolate chips

For cake: Preheat oven to 350°F. Butter 10x2-inch round cake pan. Using electric mixer, beat eggs and sugar until slowly dissolving ribbon forms when beaters are lifted. Gently fold in flour. Turn batter into prepared pan. Bake until top is springy to touch, about 20 minutes. Cool in pan.

For syrup: Cook sugar and water in heavy small saucepan over low heat until sugar dissolves, swirling pan occasionally. Increase heat and bring to boil. Remove from heat. Stir in rum. Cool completely.

For cream: Using electric mixer, beat cream with sugar to stiff peaks. Transfer half to another bowl. Fold melted chocolate into cream in mixer bowl. Fold nuts and chocolate chips into other.

To assemble: Using long serrated knife, cut cake horizontally into 4 layers. Set bottom layer in 10x3-inch springform pan. Cut 2 middle layers into 2-inch squares. Line sides of pan with squares. Brush cake with syrup. Spoon chocolate cream over bottom layer, spreading evenly. Top with nut-chocolate chip cream, spreading evenly. Place fourth layer on nut-chocolate chip cream, smooth side up.

To garnish: Set cake on platter. Remove springform. Brush top and sides generously with apricot glaze. Sprinkle with nuts and chocolate chips. Serve immediately.

Tea Cake with Lemon Custard Icing and Fresh Berries

Topped with pale yellow icing and bright berries, this is a festive and pretty dessert.

10 servings

Lemon Cake
9 egg whites, room temperature
1 teaspoon cream of tartar
⅛ teaspoon salt
5 egg yolks, room temperature
1½ cups sugar
1 cup cake flour, sifted 5 times
2½ teaspoons grated lemon peel

Custard
1 envelope unflavored gelatin
½ cup fresh lemon juice

1½ cups whipping cream
5 egg yolks, room temperature
¾ cup sugar
2 teaspoons grated lemon peel
2 cups whipping cream, beaten to soft peaks

Lemon leaves or fresh lemon balm (optional)
3 cups fresh berries (such as blueberries, raspberries, strawberries and/or currants)

For cake: Preheat oven to 200°F. Grease and flour 10-inch tube pan. Using electric mixer, beat whites until frothy. Add cream of tartar and salt and beat until whites are stiff but not dry. In another bowl beat yolks until pale yellow and thick. Gradually add sugar and beat until pale yellow and slowly dissolving ribbon forms when beaters are lifted. Gently fold half of whites into yolks, then gently fold in flour. Fold in remaining whites and lemon peel. Pour batter into prepared pan. Bake 15 minutes. Increase heat to 225°F and cook 15 minutes. Increase heat to 250°F and cook 15 minutes. Increase heat to 275°F and cook 15 minutes. Increase heat to 300°F and cook until cake is springy to touch, about 15 minutes. Cool in pan.

For custard: Sprinkle gelatin over lemon juice in small bowl. Heat 1½ cups cream in top of double boiler over simmering water. Using electric mixer, beat yolks in medium bowl until pale yellow. Gradually beat in sugar. Blend in warm cream. Return mixture to top of double boiler. Stir over medium-high heat until custard thickens and coats spoon, about 10 minutes. Mix in gelatin and lemon peel and stir until gelatin is dissolved. Refrigerate until chilled but not set. Fold in whipped cream.

Remove cake from pan and cut into 3 layers, using serrated knife. Reassemble cake, spreading each layer with generous amount of custard. Spread remaining custard over top and sides of cake. *(Can be prepared 1 day ahead. Cover and refrigerate.)*

Line platter with lemon leaves. Carefully transfer cake to platter, using 2 spatulas as aid. Spoon berries into center of cake and over leaves. Let cake stand at room temperature for 30 minutes before serving.

Coconut Cloud Cake

Use the food processor to finely shred the fresh coconut for this classic cake.

10 to 12 servings

1 medium coconut

2 cups plus 2 tablespoons cake flour
1 tablespoon baking powder
¼ teaspoon salt

3 egg whites
2 teaspoons distilled white vinegar
1¾ cups sugar

9 tablespoons unsalted butter, cut into 5 pieces, room temperature
¼ cup light rum
⅛ teaspoon almond extract
¾ cup milk

Fluffy White Frosting*

Preheat oven to 400°F. Pierce holes through coconut at 3 soft spots on one end, using hammer and nail. Drain liquid and reserve for another use. Bake coconut until shell cracks, about 20 minutes. Cool slightly. Wrap in towel. Sharply pound center of coconut with hammer to crack open. Separate meat from shell. Remove brown skin using vegetable peeler. Cut coconut into feed tube widths.

Insert fine shredder blade in processor. Arrange coconut in feed tube and shred using firm pressure. (If fine shredder is unavailable, use medium shredder. Remove shredder and carefully insert steel knife. Chop coconut coarsely using on/off turns.) Measure 2⅓ cups coconut. *(Remainder can be wrapped tightly and frozen.)*

Position rack in center of oven and preheat to 300°F. Butter two 8-inch round cake pans. Cover bottom of each pan with parchment or waxed paper; butter paper. Sift flour, baking powder and salt into small bowl.

Using steel knife, blend whites 15 seconds in clean, dry work bowl. With machine running, drizzle vinegar through feed tube and whip until whites hold shape, about 1¼ minutes. Transfer to medium bowl. Blend sugar and butter 1 minute, stopping once to scrape down sides of work bowl. With machine running, pour rum and almond extract through feed tube and mix 2 minutes. Pour milk through feed tube and mix 10 seconds. Spoon ½ cup shredded coconut in ring around inside of work bowl. Repeat with dry ingredients, then whites. Blend using 4 on/off turns. Run spatula around inside of work bowl to loosen mixture. Blend until ingredients are just combined, using 1 or 2 on/off turns. Divide batter between prepared pans. Bake until tester inserted in center comes out clean, about 45 minutes. Cool 5 minutes. Invert layers onto rack, removing paper. Cool completely. *(Can be prepared 1 day ahead. Wrap tightly and store cake layers at room temperature.)*

Place 1 cake layer upside down on platter. Slide strips of waxed paper under cake to keep plate clean. Spread ¾ cup frosting over layer. Sprinkle with ⅓ cup coconut. Top with second layer, right side up. Spread remaining frosting over top and sides of cake, using flexible metal spatula. Press 1 cup coconut into sides of cake; sprinkle ½ cup over top. Gently remove paper. *(Can be prepared 4 hours ahead.)*

*Fluffy White Frosting

Makes about 4 cups

¾ cup light corn syrup
2 egg whites
⅛ teaspoon salt

8 marshmallows, quartered
¼ teaspoon almond extract

Combine corn syrup, whites and salt in top of double boiler over gently simmering water. Beat with hand mixer until fluffy and just warm to touch, about 5 minutes. Add marshmallows and almond extract. Beat with wooden spoon until marshmallows melt, about 6 minutes. Cool until spreadable, about 20 minutes.

Hawaiian Liquor Cake

Prepare this a day early to allow the flavors to mellow. For a tropical touch, decorate the cake with fresh flowers.

12 servings

Sponge Cake
5 eggs, separated, room temperature
1 cup sugar
2 tablespoons fresh lemon juice
1 teaspoon grated lemon peel
1 teaspoon vanilla
½ teaspoon salt
¼ teaspoon cream of tartar
1 cup sifted cake flour

Pineapple Filling
5 eggs, separated, room temperature
¾ cup sugar
½ cup (1 stick) butter, melted

¼ teaspoon cream of tartar
¾ cup well-chilled whipping cream
2 20-ounce cans crushed pineapple, well drained

¼ cup crème de cacao
¼ cup apricot-flavored brandy
¼ cup white rum

3 cups well-chilled whipping cream
1 tablespoon crème de cacao
2 teaspoons sugar
Fresh pineapple slices
Maraschino cherries

For cake: Preheat oven to 325°F. Grease 9- to 10-inch tube pan. Using electric mixer, beat yolks, ½ cup sugar, lemon juice, lemon peel and vanilla until pale yellow and slowly dissolving ribbon forms when beaters are lifted. Using clean dry beaters, beat whites with salt and cream of tartar in large bowl until frothy. Add remaining ½ cup sugar 1 tablespoon at a time, beating until stiff but not dry. Gently fold yolks into whites. Fold in flour ¼ cup at a time. Turn batter into prepared pan. Bake until tester inserted in center comes out clean, 1 hour. Invert pan onto rack; cool cake in pan.

For filling: Beat yolks with ¾ cup sugar and butter until pale yellow and slowly dissolving ribbon forms when beaters are lifted. Using clean dry beaters, beat whites with cream of tartar in large bowl until stiff but not dry. Beat ¾ cup cream in another large bowl until soft peaks form. Gently fold crushed pineapple into cream. Gently fold in yolks and whites.

Remove cake from pan. Cut evenly into 3 layers. Place top layer cut side up in clean 9- to 10-inch tube pan. Sprinkle with ¼ cup crème de cacao. Spread with half of filling. Sprinkle one side of middle layer with half of apricot brandy. Arrange in pan, brandy side down. Sprinkle with remaining brandy. Spread with remaining filling. Sprinkle cut side of bottom layer with rum. Place cut side down atop filling, pressing gently. Wrap cake tightly with plastic and foil and refrigerate overnight.

Whip 3 cups cream with 1 tablespoon crème de cacao and 2 teaspoons sugar until firm peaks form. Run knife between cake and pan. Invert cake onto platter. Spread whipped cream over top and sides of cake. Garnish with pineapple slices and cherries. *(Can be prepared 1 hour ahead and refrigerated.)* Serve cake well chilled.

Laggtarta

Each light sponge layer of the Laggtarta or "frying pan cake" is baked in a skillet to make this Swedish classic.

10 servings

1 pint (2 cups) strawberries, hulled
2 tablespoons strawberry liqueur or crème de cassis

½ cup red currant jelly
½ cup thick unsweetened applesauce

3 eggs, room temperature
1 cup sugar
1 cup cake flour

1 teaspoon baking powder
½ cup (1 stick) unsalted butter, melted and clarified

1½ pints (3 cups) strawberries, finely chopped
Powdered sugar
Whipped cream

Combine 1 pint strawberries with liqueur in serving bowl and blend well. Cover and marinate at room temperature 2 hours, stirring occasionally.

Melt jelly in small saucepan over low heat, stirring until smooth. Remove from heat and cool slightly. Blend in applesauce. Refrigerate 2 hours.

Meanwhile, preheat oven to 425°F. Beat eggs in large bowl. Gradually add sugar, beating until mixture is thick and pale yellow, about 5 minutes. Sift flour and baking powder. Fold into egg mixture. Gradually fold in clarified butter, blending thoroughly.

Generously oil 8-inch ovenproof heavy aluminum skillet or omelet pan. Spread ⅙ of batter in pan. Bake until lightly browned, about 5 minutes. Gently loosen edges of cake using wide spatula or pancake turner. Ease layer out onto wire rack (using 2 spatulas if necessary). Let cool. Repeat with remaining batter for a total of 6 layers, *cleaning pan thoroughly and oiling generously each time more batter is added.*

To serve: Combine remaining 1½ pints strawberries with applesauce mixture, blending well. Spread evenly over 5 layers. Stack layers together on serving platter filled side up, topping with plain layer. Sift powdered sugar over top. Cut into wedges. Pass marinated strawberries and whipped cream.

Spekkuk Cacao

An intriguing concept in cake making: A layer of spiced batter is baked, then a layer of plain batter is poured over it and baked. The procedure is repeated until all of the batter is used.

25 servings

1 cup (2 sticks) unsalted butter, room temperature
1 cup superfine sugar
10 egg yolks

1⅓ cups sifted all purpose flour
¼ teaspoon salt
8 egg whites, room temperature
¼ teaspoon cream of tartar
¼ cup unsweetened cocoa powder, sifted

1½ teaspoons cinnamon
1 teaspoon freshly grated nutmeg
1 teaspoon ground cardamom
1 teaspoon vanilla
¼ teaspoon ground cloves

6 tablespoons melted butter

Powdered sugar

Place oven rack in lowest position and preheat to 300°F. Generously butter and flour 9-inch springform pan, shaking out excess. Cream butter in large bowl of electric mixer. Gradually add superfine sugar, beating until light and fluffy. Blend in egg yolks one at a time. Beat batter for 10 minutes.

Resift flour with salt. Stir into batter, mixing well. Beat egg whites with cream of tartar in another bowl just until stiff. Carefully fold into batter, blending thoroughly. Transfer half of batter to medium bowl. Fold in cocoa, cinnamon, freshly grated nutmeg, cardamom, vanilla and cloves.

Spread ⅛-inch-thick layer of spiced batter in bottom of prepared pan. Bake until cake tester inserted in center of cake comes out clean, about 15 minutes. Remove from oven and gently brush top of cake generously with melted butter (feather brush works best). Spread ⅛-inch-thick layer of *plain* batter over top of cooked layer.

Position rack in center of oven. Bake cake until added layer tests done, about 15 minutes. Brush top generously with melted butter. Repeat layering and baking until all batter is used (if layers bake considerably faster than 15 minutes, reduce oven temperature to 275°F), baking final layer 30 to 35 minutes, or until cake tests done. Remove springform and let cake cool completely on wire rack.

Sift powdered sugar over top of cake before serving (use stencil, doily or cardboard pattern to create decorative effect). Slice cake into thin wedges.

Loralee's Chocolate Meringue Cake

10 to 12 servings

¼ cup (½ stick) butter, room temperature
¾ cup sugar
4 egg yolks
2 ounces unsweetened chocolate, melted
2 ounces semisweet chocolate, melted
1 teaspoon vanilla
½ cup sifted all purpose flour
½ teaspoon baking soda

¼ teaspoon salt
¼ cup hot water
1 6-ounce package semisweet chocolate chips

4 egg whites, room temperature
¼ cup sugar

1 cup whipping cream
¼ cup powdered sugar
Chocolate shavings (garnish)

Preheat oven to 350°F. Grease and flour bottoms of two 8-inch round cake pans. Cream butter with ¾ cup sugar until fluffy. Beat in yolks. Add chocolates and vanilla. Stir in flour, baking soda and salt. Blend in hot water. Pour batter into pans. Sprinkle evenly with chocolate chips.

Beat whites until soft peaks form. Gradually add ¼ cup sugar and continue beating until stiff but not dry. Spread meringue over each layer, covering completely. Bake until meringue browns, about 35 minutes. Cool in pans 10 minutes, then turn out onto racks to cool. *(Frost within 6 hours.)*

Just before serving, whip cream with powdered sugar until soft peaks form. Invert one cake layer over the other so meringues are in center. Frost top and sides of cake with whipped cream. Garnish with chocolate shavings. Serve immediately.

Siren's Chocolate Cake

12 servings

Cake

Solid vegetable shortening
½ cup (1 stick) unsalted butter
4 ounces unsweetened chocolate, coarsely chopped
2 cups buttermilk
2 eggs, room temperature
2 teaspoons vanilla
2½ cups all purpose flour
2 cups sugar
2 teaspoons baking soda
1 teaspoon instant coffee powder
½ teaspoon salt

Chocolate Icing

½ cup (1 stick) unsalted butter
4 ounces unsweetened chocolate, coarsely chopped
2 teaspoons instant coffee powder
1 pound (or more) powdered sugar, sifted
½ cup evaporated milk
2 teaspoons vanilla

For cake: Preheat oven to 350°F. Grease two 9-inch round cake pans with vegetable shortening. Melt butter and chocolate in top of double boiler over gently simmering water. Stir to blend. Beat buttermilk with eggs and vanilla in large bowl of electric mixer to blend. Sift dry ingredients over top and mix in. Beat in chocolate mixture. Spoon into prepared pans. Bake until tester inserted in centers of layers comes out clean, about 30 minutes. *(Layers rise about ¾ inch above pan.)* Cool in pans on racks 15 minutes. Invert onto racks and cool completely.

For icing: Melt butter and chocolate with coffee powder in top of double boiler over gently simmering water. Stir to blend. Combine 1 pound sugar, evaporated milk and vanilla in bowl of electric mixer. Add chocolate mixture and beat until thick enough to spread, adding more powdered sugar if necessary. Spread icing evenly between layers and over tops and sides of cake. *(Cake can be prepared 1 day ahead. Store at room temperature.)*

Rich Chocolate Layer Cake

Make this luscious cake quickly and easily with the help of the processor.

10 servings

All purpose flour
1¼ cups cake flour
¾ teaspoon baking powder
½ teaspoon baking soda
½ teaspoon salt

3 eggs, separated
2 teaspoons distilled white vinegar
2 ounces unsweetened chocolate, broken into pieces
1½ cups firmly packed dark brown sugar

½ cup strong boiling-hot coffee
2 tablespoons unsweetened cocoa powder
½ cup (1 stick) unsalted butter, quartered, room temperature
½ cup sour cream
2 tablespoons coffee liqueur or vanilla

3 tablespoons apricot preserves, melted
Chocolate Cream Frosting*

Position rack in center of oven and preheat to 350°F. Butter two 8-inch round cake pans; dust with flour. Sift cake flour, baking powder, baking soda and salt into medium bowl.

Blend whites 15 seconds in processor in clean, dry work bowl. With machine running, drizzle vinegar through feed tube and whip until whites hold shape, about 1¼ minutes. Transfer to another medium bowl. Chop chocolate with ½ cup brown sugar using 6 on/off turns, then process continuously until chocolate is finely minced, about 30 seconds. With machine running, pour hot coffee through feed tube and blend 20 seconds, stopping once to scrape down sides of work bowl. Add yolks, remaining 1 cup sugar and cocoa and mix 1 minute. Add butter and blend 1 minute. Add sour cream and liqueur and mix 5 seconds. Spoon dry ingredients in ring around inside of work bowl. Repeat with whites. Blend using 2 on/off turns. Run spatula around inside of work bowl to loosen mixture. Blend until ingredients are just combined, using 2 or 3 on/off turns. Divide batter between prepared pans. Bake until tester inserted in center comes out clean, about 35 minutes. Cool 5 minutes. Invert layers onto rack and cool completely.

Press preserves through fine sieve. Place 1 cake layer upside down on platter. Slide strips of waxed paper under cake to keep plate clean. Spread preserves over cake. Top with second layer, right side up. Spread chocolate frosting over top and sides of cake using flexible metal spatula. *(Can be prepared 2 days ahead. Cover cake tightly and store at room temperature.)*

*Chocolate Cream Frosting

Makes about 1½ cups

3 ounces sweet cooking chocolate, broken into pieces
6 tablespoons (¾ stick) unsalted butter, melted and still hot
2½ cups powdered sugar

5 to 6 tablespoons sour cream
1 tablespoon coffee liqueur or vanilla
Pinch of salt

Chop chocolate in processor using 5 on/off turns, then process continuously until finely minced. With machine running, pour hot butter through feed tube and blend until chocolate is melted, stopping once to scrape down sides of work bowl. Add powdered sugar, 5 tablespoons sour cream, coffee liqueur and salt. Mix until smooth. If frosting is too thick, add 1 tablespoon sour cream and blend 5 seconds.

Chocolate Cake with Blueberries

10 to 12 servings

Génoise
5 eggs
½ cup plus 2 tablespoons sugar
½ cup plus 2 tablespoons all purpose flour
3½ teaspoons unsweetened cocoa powder
2 tablespoons (¼ stick) unsalted butter, melted

Blueberry Filling
3 cups fresh blueberries
¾ cup sugar
3 tablespoons fresh lemon juice
1½ tablespoons dark rum

Ganache
1 pound semisweet chocolate, coarsely chopped
2 cups whipping cream
1½ tablespoons dark rum

1 cup fresh blueberries (garnish)
Chocolate leaves (optional decoration)

For génoise: Preheat oven to 350°F. Butter and flour two 8-inch round cake pans. Blend eggs and sugar in large bowl of electric mixer. Set bowl over pan of barely simmering water and whisk until very warm to touch. Transfer bowl to mixer and beat until mixture is thick and has nearly tripled in volume, 8 to 10 minutes. Sift together flour and cocoa. Resift ⅓ of dry ingredients over egg mixture; fold in gently. Repeat with remaining dry ingredients. Fold small amount of batter into melted butter. Gently fold mixture back into remaining batter; do not overfold or cake will be heavy.

Divide batter between prepared pans. Bake until cake begins to pull away from sides of pan and top springs back when lightly touched, 25 to 30 minutes. Cool layers in pans 10 minutes. Invert layers onto wire rack. *(Can be prepared 1 day ahead. Wrap in plastic and store at room temperature.)*

For filling: Cook 3 cups blueberries, sugar and lemon juice in heavy saucepan over medium heat, stirring until sugar dissolves. Increase heat slightly and simmer 10 minutes, mashing berries into juice. Cool 5 minutes. Add rum. *(Blueberry filling can be prepared 1 day ahead and refrigerated. Bring to room temperature before using.)*

For ganache: Bring chocolate and cream to boil in heavy medium saucepan over medium-low heat, stirring occasionally. Cool until mixture begins to thicken and set, stirring occasionally, about 35 minutes. Transfer to bowl of electric mixer. Add rum and beat at high speed until mixture lightens in color and almost doubles in volume, 4 to 5 minutes. (Ganache must be used immediately or it will harden.)

To assemble: Split each cake layer in half using long serrated knife. *Without stacking layers,* cover 3 layers evenly with filling, then top each generously with ganache, reserving remainder for top and sides. Stack frosted layers, placing unfrosted layer on top. Frost top and sides quickly with remaining ganache. Refrigerate. Let stand at room temperature 30 minutes before serving. Garnish with remaining 1 cup blueberries. Decorate top of cake with chocolate leaves if desired.

 Rolled Cakes

Coffee Sponge Roll with Double Fudge Mocha Filling

Quickly prepare the cake and filling in the processor.

10 servings

¾ cup cake flour
1½ teaspoons baking powder
⅛ teaspoon salt

3 eggs, separated
1 teaspoon distilled white vinegar
¾ cup sugar

¼ cup hot strong brewed coffee

8 tablespoons powdered sugar

Fudge Mocha Filling*
1 cup whipping cream, whipped
Lightly toasted sliced almonds

Position rack in center of oven and preheat to 375°F. Butter 12x18-inch jelly roll pan. Line with waxed paper, leaving 2-inch overhang beyond edge of short sides. Butter paper. Sift cake flour, baking powder and salt into small bowl. Set aside.

Blend egg whites in processor 8 seconds. With machine running, pour vinegar through feed tube and process until whites are stiff and hold their shape, about 2 minutes. Transfer to small bowl, using rubber spatula (do not clean work bowl). Combine yolks and ¾ cup sugar in work bowl and mix 1 minute. With machine running, pour hot coffee through feed tube and blend 10 seconds. Spoon flour mixture over. Top with whites. Blend using 2 on/off turns. Run spatula around inside of work bowl. Blend just until whites are combined, using 2 to 3 on/off turns (some streaks of white may remain; do not overprocess).

Spread batter in prepared pan. Bake until light brown and set, about 10 minutes. Sift 1 tablespoon powdered sugar over top of cake. Top with piece of waxed paper, then cover with slightly dampened towel. Invert onto rack. Carefully peel off paper; cover with dry towel. Let cool 30 minutes. *(Can be prepared 2 days ahead. Roll up in dry towel and refrigerate.)*

To assemble: Spread 1½ cups filling over cake. Gently fold remaining filling into whipped cream. Spread mixture over filling. Roll up as for jelly roll, starting at 1 short edge, using bottom towel as aid and removing waxed paper. Carefully transfer cake to platter, arranging seam side down. Refrigerate at least 2 hours. Let stand at room temperature 30 minutes before serving. Sift remaining 7 tablespoons powdered sugar over top. Decorate cake with toasted sliced almonds. Slice cake on slight diagonal.

*Fudge Mocha Filling

Makes about 2 cups

6 tablespoons (¾ stick) unsalted butter, room temperature
¼ cup strong brewed coffee

4 ounces unsweetened chocolate, broken into pieces

2 cups powdered sugar
3 tablespoons sour cream
1½ teaspoons vanilla

Melt 2 tablespoons butter with coffee in small saucepan; keep at simmer.

Chop chocolate in processor with ½ cup sugar using 6 on/off turns, then process continuously until chocolate is finely ground. With machine running, pour hot butter mixture through feed tube and process until chocolate is melted and smooth, stopping once to scrape down sides of work bowl. Cut remaining 4 tablespoons butter into 4 pieces. Add butter pieces, remaining 1½ cups sugar, sour cream and vanilla and mix until smooth, stopping as necessary to scrape down sides of work bowl. *(Can be prepared 4 days ahead, covered and refrigerated. Return filling to processor and blend until soft enough to spread. Use steel knife.)*

Chocolate Raspberry Cloud Roll

One-half cup purchased raspberry jelly mixed with 1 teaspoon fresh lemon juice can be substituted for the Raspberry Jam Cordon Rose. Reduce sugar in cream recipe to ¼ cup.

10 to 12 servings

Chocolate Nut Roll
6 eggs, separated, room temperature
10 tablespoons sugar
4 ounces extra bittersweet or semisweet chocolate, melted and cooled
½ cup almonds, ground
¼ teaspoon cream of tartar
2 tablespoons sugar

Raspberry Cloud Cream
3 egg yolks, room temperature

6 tablespoons sugar
¼ cup light corn syrup

1 cup (2 sticks) unsalted butter, room temperature
¼ cup Raspberry Jam Cordon Rose*
1 tablespoon framboise (raspberry eau-de-vie)
6 drops red food coloring (optional)

Unsweetened cocoa powder
Sifted powdered sugar
16 Chocolate Leaves**
1 ounce extra bittersweet or semisweet chocolate, melted
4 raspberries

For nut roll: Position rack in lower third of oven and preheat to 350°F. Oil 17x11-inch jelly roll pan. Line with parchment or waxed paper, allowing paper to extend over edges. Grease and flour paper. Using electric mixer, beat yolks and 10 tablespoons sugar until pale yellow and slowly dissolving ribbon forms when beaters are lifted. Beat in chocolate, then nuts. Beat whites and cream of tartar in another bowl until soft peaks form. Gradually add 2 tablespoons sugar, beating until stiff but not dry. Gently fold ¼ of whites into chocolate mixture to lighten, then fold in remaining whites. Pour into prepared pan, spreading evenly. Bake until cake puffs and loses its shine, 18 minutes. Remove cake from oven. Immediately cover with damp towel. Set aside and allow to cool completely.

For raspberry cream: Using electric mixer, beat yolks until light.

Meanwhile, heat sugar and corn syrup in heavy small saucepan over low heat, swirling pan occasionally, until sugar dissolves. Increase heat and boil until candy thermometer registers 236°F (soft-ball stage). Immediately beat syrup into yolks in thin stream. Beat until cool. Gradually add butter, beating until smooth and creamy. Beat in raspberry jam. Mix in framboise and coloring. *(Can be prepared 4 hours ahead and stored at room temperature or 1 day ahead and refrigerated. Bring to room temperature before continuing. Rebeat if necessary to restore texture.)*

Uncover chocolate roll. Sift cocoa over surface. Invert onto towel and remove waxed paper. Spread raspberry cream over cake, leaving ½-inch border. Roll cake up jelly roll fashion, starting at 17-inch side. Roll onto serving platter, seam side down, removing towel; cake may crack. *(Can be prepared 1 day ahead; wrap tightly and refrigerate.)* Sift cocoa over top of cake, then dust with powdered sugar. Arrange chocolate leaves atop cake in clusters of 4, using melted chocolate to attach. Garnish with whole fresh raspberries.

*Raspberry Jam Cordon Rose

Tart and intensely flavored, a perfect showcase for the season's best berries.

Makes 5½ cups

3 cups sugar
1½ cups water

4 pounds raspberries

Cook sugar and water in heavy 8- to 10-quart saucepan over low heat, swirling pan occasionally, until sugar dissolves. Increase heat and boil 1 minute. Add enough berries to form single layer in pan. Boil 1 minute. Transfer berries to strainer set over medium bowl, using slotted spoon. Boil syrup until reduced to original volume. Repeat with remaining berries, returning syrup from bowl to pan. Boil syrup until candy thermometer registers 220°F, about 15 minutes.

Press berries through strainer, discarding seeds. Mix berries into syrup. Reduce heat and simmer until reduced to 5½ cups, stirring frequently near end of cooking.

Rinse canning jars with boiling water. Spoon boiling hot jam into jars to ¼ inch from top. Immediately wipe rim of jars and seal. Arrange jars on rack in large pot. Cover with boiling water by 1 inch. Cover pot and boil 10 minutes.

Remove jars from water bath. Cool to room temperature. Press center of each lid for tight seal. If lid stays down, jar is sealed. Store in cool dry place for up to 1 year. Refrigerate after opening. (If lid pops up, store jam in refrigerator.)

**Chocolate Leaves

Makes about 16

3 ounces summer coating, compound chocolate or semisweet chocolate, chopped

16 small thick leaves such as rose, camellia or gardenia, with ⅛ inch of stem

Melt chocolate in top of double boiler over hot water. Stir until smooth. Spread in thin layer over veined side of leaves, being careful not to drip on edges. Refrigerate until firm. Gently peel off leaves, starting at stem end.

Hazelnut Roulade

8 servings

Hazelnut Sponge Cake
½ cup (scant) hazelnuts, toasted and husked
2 tablespoons sugar
1 cup sifted cake flour

6 eggs, room temperature
¾ cup sugar

Powdered sugar

Whipped Cream Filling
½ teaspoon unflavored gelatin
1 tablespoon cold water
½ teaspoon vanilla
1 cup well-chilled whipping cream
3 tablespoons powdered sugar

Hazelnut Praline Buttercream
½ cup (1 stick) well-chilled unsalted butter, cut into 6 pieces

1¼ cups powdered sugar
¼ teaspoon instant coffee powder
1 teaspoon brandy
2 egg yolks
1 teaspoon whipping cream (or more)
⅓ cup Hazelnut Praline*

Hazelnut Praline
8 hazelnuts, toasted and husked

For cake: Preheat oven to 350°F. Butter bottom of 10x15-inch jelly roll pan. Line with parchment; butter paper. Finely chop hazelnuts with 2 tablespoons sugar in processor. Transfer to small bowl. Mix in flour.

Combine eggs and ¾ cup sugar in large bowl of electric mixer. Whisk over pan of simmering water until very warm to touch, about 4 minutes. Beat with mixer until tripled in volume, about 10 minutes. Gently fold in nut mixture. Pour batter into prepared pan, smoothing top. Bake until cake is golden brown and center is springy to touch, 18 to 20 minutes.

Dust 14x22-inch kitchen towel generously with powdered sugar. Cut around sides of cake using small spatula. Immediately invert cake onto sugared towel. Remove parchment. Dust cake with powdered sugar. Fold one end of towel over 10-inch side of cake and roll up jelly roll fashion, starting at 10-inch end. Allow to cool completely.

For filling: Soften gelatin in water in small bowl. Set bowl in pan of simmering water and stir until gelatin is dissolved. Add vanilla. Using electric mixer, whip cream until soft peaks form. Beat in sugar and gelatin mixture; continue beating until stiff peaks form. Cover and refrigerate while preparing buttercream.

For buttercream: Soften butter at room temperature 30 minutes.

Mix powdered sugar in processor to remove any lumps. Arrange butter atop sugar in circle. Process until mixture forms ball, about 20 seconds. Dissolve coffee in brandy in small bowl. Mix yolks and 1 teaspoon cream into brandy. With machine running, pour liquid ingredients through feed tube and process until well mixed, 15 to 20 seconds. Scrape down sides of work bowl. Add ⅓ cup praline and blend 5 seconds. If necessary, thin buttercream to spreadable consistency with more cream, adding ½ teaspoon at a time and blending for 5 seconds.

To assemble: Unroll cake (do not flatten completely). Spread with filling. Reroll cake. Arrange seam side down on baking sheet. Spread top and sides with buttercream, leaving ends unfrosted. Sprinkle cake with praline and top with hazelnuts. Refrigerate until frosting is set, at least 3 hours. *(Can be prepared 1 day ahead.)* Trim ends. Let cake stand at room temperature 15 minutes before serving.

*Hazelnut Praline

Makes about 2 cups

½ cup sugar
2 tablespoons water

½ cup (scant) hazelnuts, toasted and husked

Oil baking sheet. Heat sugar and water in heavy small saucepan over low heat, swirling pan occasionally, until sugar dissolves. Increase heat and bring to boil, washing down sides of pan with pastry brush dipped in cold water. Boil until syrup turns deep golden brown. Mix in nuts. Immediately pour onto prepared sheet. Cool completely.

Break praline into pieces. Pulverize in processor. *(Can be prepared 3 weeks ahead. Refrigerate in airtight container.)*

Lemon-Lime Roll

This cake is pleasantly tart and refreshing.

8 servings

Lemon-Lime Filling
5 egg yolks, room temperature
⅔ cup sugar
3 tablespoons fresh lemon juice
3 tablespoons fresh lime juice
3 tablespoons water
2 tablespoons potato starch
2½ teaspoons grated lemon peel
2½ teaspoons grated lime peel
¼ cup (½ stick) butter, cut into small pieces

Meringue Frosting
⅔ cup sugar
1 egg white
2 tablespoons water

1 tablespoon fresh lemon or lime juice
1 teaspoon mild honey
Pinch of salt
½ teaspoon vanilla (optional)

Cake
4 eggs, separated, room temperature
Pinch of salt
4 tablespoons sugar
1 tablespoon grated lemon peel
¼ cup potato starch
¼ cup matzo cake meal

2 teaspoons grated lemon peel

For filling: Mix yolks, sugar, juices, water, potato starch and grated peels in heavy small saucepan. Add butter and boil over medium-low heat until mixture is very thick and pulls away from sides of pan, stirring constantly, about 1 minute. Transfer to bowl. Place plastic wrap directly on surface to prevent skin from forming. Cool filling completely. *(Can be prepared 1 day ahead and refrigerated.)*

For frosting: Using electric mixer, beat sugar, white, water, lemon juice, honey and salt in metal bowl 1 minute. Set bowl over (but not in) saucepan of briskly simmering water; do not let water touch bottom of bowl. Beat at high speed until mixture forms fairly stiff peaks and is spreadable, about 4 minutes. Remove bowl from over water and beat mixture until cool and texture of marshmallow fluff, about 3 minutes, adding vanilla if desired. Cover and cool completely. *(Meringue Frosting can be prepared 1 day ahead and refrigerated.)*

For cake: Preheat oven to 400°F. Grease bottom of 15½x10½-inch jelly roll pan. Line pan with waxed paper; grease paper. Using electric mixer, beat whites and salt in large bowl until soft peaks form. Add sugar 1 tablespoon at a time and beat until stiff but not dry. Blend yolks and 1 tablespoon lemon peel in medium bowl. Gently fold in ¼ of whites. Fold mixture back into whites. Sift potato starch and cake meal over and fold gently. Turn batter into prepared pan, spreading evenly. Bake until light brown, about 10 minutes. Run knife around side of cake to loosen and invert onto towel-lined rack. Cool completely.

To assemble: Stir ⅓ cup of frosting into filling to lighten. Mix 2 teaspoons lemon peel into remaining frosting. Discard paper from cake. Spread cake evenly with filling. Roll up tightly as for jelly roll, starting at 1 short end and using towel as aid. Transfer cake to platter, seam side down. Spread frosting over entire cake. *(Can be prepared 8 hours ahead. Tent loosely with foil and refrigerate. Bring cake roll to room temperature before serving.)*

Fresh Strawberry Cake Roll

The light, tender sponge cake is prepared in three easy steps using the food processor.

12 servings

Cake
¾ cup cake flour
1½ teaspoons baking powder
Pinch of salt

3 eggs, separated
1 tablespoon distilled white vinegar
3 tablespoons water

¾ cup sugar
1 tablespoon frozen orange juice concentrate
1 tablespoon powdered sugar

Filling and Frosting
1 pint large strawberries, hulled
2 tablespoons Grand Marnier

1 to 2 tablespoons sugar (depending on sweetness of berries)

1 envelope unflavored gelatin
¼ cup cold water
2 cups whipping cream
⅓ cup sugar
1 tablespoon Grand Marnier
1 teaspoon vanilla

½ cup raspberry jelly, melted

For cake: Line 11x17-inch jelly roll pan with waxed paper, extending paper 2 inches beyond edges of pan. Butter paper; dust lightly with flour, shaking off excess. Position rack in center of oven and preheat to 375°F. Sift flour with baking powder and salt.

Place egg whites in processor work bowl and turn machine on. After 8 seconds, pour in vinegar and 1 tablespoon water and process until egg whites are whipped and hold their shape, about 70 seconds. Using rubber spatula, gently transfer whites to 1-quart mixing bowl. Do not wash work bowl.

Combine egg yolks, sugar, orange juice concentrate and remaining 2 tablespoons water in work bowl and blend 1 minute. Add flour mixture in ring around inside of work bowl. Spoon egg whites onto flour. Blend using 2 on/off turns; scrape down sides of work bowl. Process with 2 to 3 more on/off turns just until batter is mixed (some streaks of egg white may remain; do not overprocess). Using rubber spatula, spread batter evenly in prepared pan. Tap pan lightly on counter to remove air bubbles. Bake until lightly browned, 12 to 14 minutes. Sift powdered sugar evenly over top. Cover cake with piece of waxed paper, then with dampened towel. Invert cake onto paper and towel. Remove pan. Let cake stand until cool, about 30 minutes. Carefully peel off top sheet of waxed paper. Cover cake with piece of foil. Invert cake onto foil. Cover cake with waxed paper and towel until ready to roll.

For filling and frosting: Insert thick or medium slicer. Reserve 6 perfect strawberries for garnish. Slice remaining berries using light pressure. Transfer to small mixing bowl. Add 2 tablespoons Grand Marnier and 1 to 2 tablespoons sugar to berries and toss gently. Marinate 20 minutes. Drain well.

Sprinkle gelatin over water in 1-cup measure and let stand until all water is absorbed. Set cup in pan of hot water and stir until gelatin is dissolved. Whip cream in large bowl, gradually adding ⅓ cup sugar, until stiff. Stir in 1 tablespoon Grand Marnier with vanilla. Gently fold in dissolved gelatin, blending thoroughly. Set 1½ cups mixture aside for frosting. Fold drained berries into remaining cream.

To assemble: Remove towel and waxed paper from cake. Spread jelly evenly over top of cake. Starting at short end of roll, spoon ⅓ of strawberry-whipped cream mixture in strip about 3 inches in from end of cake. Gently roll up cake, making 1 complete turn to cover berry mixture. Repeat twice with remaining strawberry mixture; finish rolling cake. Carefully transfer roll seam side down to platter. Spread reserved whipped cream mixture over roll using flexible-blade spatula, making small decorative peaks. Halve reserved strawberries and arrange over top. Chill until ready to serve.

Praline and Pear Cake Roll

8 servings

Praline
½ cup plus 1 tablespoon sugar
2½ ounces (½ cup) blanched almonds, toasted

Cake Roll
⅓ cup unsweetened cocoa powder
2 tablespoons cake flour
1 teaspoon instant coffee powder
⅛ teaspoon freshly grated nutmeg
5 eggs
2 egg yolks
¾ cup sugar

Powdered sugar

Buttercream
4 egg yolks
½ cup sugar
1 cup half and half, scalded
1½ teaspoons vanilla
2 tablespoons praline liqueur or amaretto liqueur
1¼ cups (2½ sticks) unsalted butter, room temperature

Glaze
1 11-ounce jar pear preserves
1 tablespoon kirsch

Chocolate curls

For praline: Cook sugar in heavy small skillet over low heat until dissolved, swirling pan occasionally. Increase heat and cook until sugar turns dark brown. Stir in nuts. Pour nut mixture onto oiled baking sheet. Cool completely. Break into pieces. Finely grind in processor.

For roll: Position rack in center of oven and preheat to 350°F. Line baking sheet with foil. Grease and flour foil, shaking off excess. Sift together cocoa powder, flour, coffee and nutmeg. Beat eggs and yolks with ¾ cup sugar in large bowl of electric mixer until light and fluffy. Fold in dry ingredients in 2 additions. Pour batter onto prepared sheet, spreading evenly. Bake until edges are dry, about 15 minutes.

Meanwhile, line work surface with waxed paper. Dust with powdered sugar. Invert roll onto paper. Peel off foil. Cover with damp towel. Starting at short end, loosely roll up paper, cake and towel as for jelly roll. Let cool 15 minutes. Unroll and remove towel.

For buttercream: Whisk yolks with sugar in double boiler until well blended. Whisk in half and half. Set over simmering water and stir with wooden spoon until custard thickens, about 8 minutes. Remove from over water. Blend in vanilla. Set in bowl filled with water and ice. Let cool, stirring occasionally. Mix in liqueur. Beat butter in large bowl of electric mixer until light and fluffy. Beat in custard. Transfer to metal bowl. Hold bowl over very low heat and beat with wooden spoon until softened and homogenized, 1 to 2 minutes. Fold in praline. Refrigerate 20 minutes.

For glaze: Heat preserves and kirsch in heavy small saucepan over low heat until preserves melt, stirring occasionally. Puree in processor until smooth. Transfer to small bowl and refrigerate until glaze begins to thicken.

To assemble: Spread cake with half of buttercream. Cover with glaze. Starting at short end, roll cake up as for jelly roll, removing waxed paper as you roll. Transfer to platter. Frost with remaining buttercream. Trim ends. Decorate with chocolate curls. Refrigerate 30 minutes before serving.

3 ❧ Ice Cream and Frozen Cakes

No two foods go together better than ice cream and cake. They're a delicious combination of tastes and textures that appeals to everyone, no matter what age. So what could be more perfect than an ice cream cake? These frozen treats are unusual, refreshing and easy to make. And they are the ideal do-ahead dessert: You can make them well in advance, pop them in the freezer and forget about them until serving time.

Our selection includes a simple but colorful Peach-Pecan Ice Cream Cake (page 50), topped with sliced fresh peaches and an apricot glaze; a spectacular Tropical Ice Cream Dome (page 51), fresh apricot mousse within a shell of coconut chiffon cake and coconut ice cream; and Queen of Sheba Ice Cream Cake (page 59), with layers of cocoa-almond cake, rich chocolate parfait and chocolate whipped cream. Many of the recipes call for homemade ice cream, but if you want to save time, you can usually substitute a good-quality storebought brand.

In addition to ice cream cakes, this chapter includes less traditional frozen desserts, such as Frozen Lemon and Meringue Cake (page 52), a Frozen Fudge Cake with Brandied Cream (page 56) and Frozen Chocolate Mousse Cake with Candied Fruit and Chartreuse (page 62). These also need to be made ahead of time and frozen; but be sure to note that, in many cases, the dessert requires some time in the refrigerator to soften before it is served.

Apricots and Cream Cake

8 to 10 servings

Sponge Cake
⅓ cup milk
1 tablespoon butter

¾ cup sifted all purpose flour
1¼ teaspoons baking powder
Pinch of salt
2 eggs, room temperature
¾ cup sugar
½ teaspoon vanilla
½ teaspoon almond extract

Filling
⅔ cup dried apricots
½ teaspoon cinnamon

⅛ teaspoon freshly grated nutmeg
1 quart French vanilla ice cream, softened

3 tablespoons apricot brandy

½ cup apricot jam
3 tablespoons water
1 cup toasted slivered almonds
2 14-ounce cans apricot halves, drained

For cake: Heat milk in heavy small saucepan until bubbles begin to appear on surface. Remove from heat. Add butter and stir to melt. Cool.

Preheat oven to 350°F. Grease 9-inch cake pan. Line bottom with parchment paper. Sift flour, baking powder and salt into small bowl. Using electric mixer, beat eggs and sugar until slowly dissolving ribbon forms when beaters are lifted. Gently fold in flour. Gently fold in milk mixture, vanilla and almond extract. Pour batter into prepared pan. Bake until pale golden and springy to touch, 22 to 25 minutes. Cool in pan 5 minutes. Invert onto rack and cool completely. Wrap in plastic and freeze until ready to use. *(Can be prepared 2 weeks ahead.)*

For filling: Combine dried apricots with water to cover in heavy small saucepan and bring to boil. Reduce heat and simmer until tender, 10 to 12 minutes. Drain well. Cut into slivers. Transfer to small bowl. Toss with cinnamon and nutmeg. Fold apricots into ice cream, using wooden spoon.

To assemble: Split cake into 2 layers. Set 1 layer on platter. Drizzle with apricot brandy. Spread with ice cream mixture. Top with second cake layer. Freeze until ready to glaze and serve.

Heat jam and water in heavy small saucepan over low heat, stirring constantly. Brush glaze over top and sides of cake. Press almonds onto sides. Arrange apricot halves over top. Brush with glaze. Serve immediately.

Peach-Pecan Ice Cream Cake

6 to 8 servings

Pecan Crust
1⅔ cups pecan halves
2½ tablespoons powdered sugar
Pinch of salt
2½ tablespoons unsalted butter, room temperature

2 pints peach ice cream

Apricot Glaze
2½ tablespoons apricot preserves
1 teaspoon fresh lemon juice

1 teaspoon sugar
1 teaspoon water

1 medium peach, peeled and thinly sliced
Mint sprigs

For crust: Preheat oven to 350°F. Lightly butter 9-inch ovenproof glass pie dish. Finely chop pecans with sugar and salt in processor, using on/off turns; do not mix to powder. Stir in butter using fork. Press mixture evenly into prepared pan. Bake until light brown, about 8 minutes. Cool completely on rack. Freeze 10 minutes.

Soften ice cream in refrigerator until spreadable. Smooth into crust, mounding slightly in center. Freeze until firm, about 2 hours. *(Can be prepared up to 1 week ahead. Cover tightly.)*

For glaze: Melt preserves with lemon juice, sugar and water in heavy small saucepan over low heat, stirring frequently. Strain mixture.

Arrange peach slices in flower pattern in center of cake. Brush peaches with glaze. Garnish with mint. Let soften in refrigerator for 10 minutes before serving.

Tropical Ice Cream Dome

This spectacular dessert has a fresh apricot mousse and coconut ice cream in the center.

12 servings

Coconut Chiffon Cake
- ¾ cup sifted cake flour
- 1½ teaspoons baking powder
- ½ teaspoon salt
- ¾ cup sugar
- ¼ cup vegetable oil
- 3 egg yolks, room temperature
- 6 tablespoons cold water
- 1 teaspoon vanilla

- 4 egg whites, room temperature
- ¼ teaspoon cream of tartar
- ¾ cup finely grated dried unsweetened coconut*

Coconut Ice Cream
- 2 pints vanilla ice cream
- 1 cup finely grated dried unsweetened coconut

Peach Brandy Syrup
- ¼ cup sugar
- ¼ cup water
- 2 tablespoons peach brandy

Apricot Mousse
- 5 ounces unpeeled ripe apricots, halved and cut into 1-inch pieces

- ⅔ cup sugar
- ½ cup water

- 2 egg whites, room temperature
  Pinch of cream of tartar

- ¾ cup plus 2 tablespoons whipping cream, well chilled

- 3 tablespoons finely grated dried unsweetened coconut, toasted
- 2 ripe apricots, thinly sliced

For cake: Position rack in center of oven and preheat to 400°F. Lightly butter corners of 11x14¾-inch rimmed baking sheet. Line with parchment; butter paper. Resift flour with baking powder and salt into large bowl. Stir in ½ cup sugar. Make well in center of mixture. Blend oil, yolks, water and vanilla in well with spoon. Gradually stir in dry ingredients until smooth.

Beat whites with cream of tartar using electric mixer until soft peaks form. Add remaining 4 tablespoons sugar 1 tablespoon at a time and beat until stiff and shiny. Fold ¼ of whites into yolk mixture to lighten. Fold yolk mixture into remaining whites until almost blended. Fold in ¾ cup coconut. Turn batter onto prepared sheet, smoothing lightly. Bake until just firm, springy to touch and beginning to brown, about 6 minutes. Transfer cake with paper to rack. Cover with towel and allow to cool completely.

For ice cream: Soften ice cream slightly in refrigerator. Mix in coconut. Freeze until firm, about 30 minutes.

For syrup: Heat sugar and water in heavy small saucepan over low heat, swirling pan until sugar dissolves. Increase heat and bring mixture to boil. Cool completely. Stir in brandy.

Lightly oil 10-cup metal bowl. Freeze until well chilled. Soften ice cream in refrigerator until just spreadable. Spread evenly over inside of chilled bowl, up to rim. Freeze until firm, about 30 minutes. (If ice cream slips down sides of bowl, push back up with back of spoon and freeze 15 minutes longer.)

Trim hard edges of cake; remove paper. Cut ⅔ of cake crosswise into 1½-inch strips. Reserve remaining cake. Press strips into ice cream, covering completely. Brush with half of syrup. Cover and freeze at least 15 minutes.

For mousse: Puree apricots in processor until very smooth. Measure ⅔ cup.

Heat sugar and water in heavy small saucepan over low heat, swirling pan until sugar dissolves. Increase heat and boil, *without stirring,* until thermometer registers 238°F (soft-ball stage).

Meanwhile, beat whites and cream of tartar with electric mixer until stiff but not dry. Add hot syrup in thin stream, beating at high speed until mixture is cool and shiny. Fold in apricot puree. Refrigerate at least 30 minutes.

Whip cream to soft peaks. Fold into apricot mixture. Pour mousse into cake-lined bowl. Freeze until firm on top, about 1 hour. Cut remaining cake to cover mousse; arrange over top. Brush with remaining peach brandy syrup. Cover and freeze at least 8 hours.

To serve, run knife around edge of dessert. Dip bowl in lukewarm water 10 seconds; pat dry. Invert onto serving platter. Shake bowl downward once. (If dessert remains in mold, dip towel in hot water, wring dry and use to cover mold until dessert releases.) Freeze 5 minutes. Smooth top with spatula. Sprinkle with coconut. Arrange apricot slices around base.

*Available at natural foods stores.

Frozen Lemon and Meringue Cake

All of the components for this spectacular cake can be prepared ahead, and the dessert itself can be assembled the day before serving and frozen.

10 to 12 servings

Swiss Meringue
- 5 egg whites, room temperature
  Pinch of cream of tartar
- 1½ cups superfine sugar

Lemon Filling
- 1 cup sugar
- 11 tablespoons unsalted butter
- ½ cup strained fresh lemon juice
- 3 eggs
- 3 egg yolks
- 1 tablespoon finely grated lemon peel

Génoise
- 3 eggs
- ½ cup sugar
- ½ teaspoon vanilla
- ½ cup sifted cake flour
- 3 tablespoons clarified butter

Simple Syrup
- 3 tablespoons water
- 2 tablespoons sugar

- 2 cups rich vanilla ice cream, softened

Preheat oven to 150°F. Line 2 baking sheets with parchment paper. Draw two 8-inch circles on 1 baking sheet. Turn parchment paper over.

For meringue: Beat whites and cream of tartar until stiff peaks form. Gradually add ¾ cup superfine sugar, beating until whites are very shiny. Gently fold in remaining sugar 1 tablespoon at a time. Spoon meringue into pastry bag fitted with ½-inch plain tip. Pipe meringue in tight 8-inch spiral beginning in center of 1 parchment circle. Repeat on second circle.

On second sheet, pipe remaining meringue into several 2-inch-high S shapes and 2½-inch-long strips. Bake meringues until crisp and dry, 2 to 3 hours; do not brown. (Or if gas oven has pilot light, meringues can be left in cold oven overnight to bake.) Remove from paper and cool on rack. Trim meringues to form 2 perfect 8-inch circles. *(Can be prepared 1 day ahead. Store at room temperature in airtight container.)*

For filling: Whisk all ingredients in top of nonaluminum double boiler set over boiling water until mixture thickens enough to coat back of spoon, about 15 minutes; do not let mixture boil. Transfer to nonaluminum container. Cool to room temperature. Cover and refrigerate until ready to use; filling should be very cold and stiff before using. *(Can be prepared up to 2 weeks ahead and refrigerated.)*

For génoise: Preheat oven to 350°F. Line 8-inch round cake pan with parchment paper; butter and flour paper. Whisk eggs and sugar in large mixer bowl set over large saucepan of gently simmering water until mixture feels warm to touch (about 100°F). Remove from heat and beat with electric mixer until slowly dissolving ribbon forms when beaters are lifted. Blend in vanilla. Resift flour over mixture in 3 batches, folding quickly and carefully after each. Blend 2 tablespoons batter into butter to lighten. Fold mixture back into remaining batter with a few strokes; do not overfold or batter will be heavy. Pour into prepared pan. Bake until cake begins to pull away from sides of pan and top feels springy to touch, 20 to 25 minutes. Invert onto rack and cool. *(Can be prepared 2 days ahead and stored at room temperature.)*

For syrup: Cook water and sugar in heavy small saucepan over low heat until sugar dissolves, swirling pan occasionally. Increase heat and bring to boil. Cool to room temperature.

To assemble: Cut cardboard circle slightly smaller than meringue circle. Set 1 meringue on top. Spread about ⅔ cup filling over; freeze until firm, about 30 minutes. Gently cover with 1 cup ice cream. Freeze 5 minutes to firm. Cut génoise in half horizontally. Wrap half and freeze for another use. Press remaining half over ice cream. Brush generously with some of syrup; do not soak. Spread about ¼ cup filling over cake; freeze until firm, about 30 minutes. Cover with remaining ice cream; freeze until firm, about 30 minutes. Spread about ⅔ cup filling over. Press remaining meringue circle on top. Smooth sides of cake; freeze until sides are firm, about 30 minutes. Spread remaining filling on sides of cake, smoothing carefully; no cake should be visible. Press meringue decorations into sides of cake. Freeze until ready to serve. *(Can be prepared 1 day ahead.)*

To serve, thaw cake in refrigerator 20 minutes. Cut with serrated knife using gentle back-and-forth motion to prevent cracking meringue.

Strawberry Sherbet Jelly Roll Loaf

6 servings

⅓ cup milk
1 tablespoon butter

¾ cup sifted all purpose flour
1¼ teaspoons baking powder
Pinch of salt
2 eggs, room temperature
¾ cup sugar
1 teaspoon vanilla

Powdered sugar

¾ cup strawberry jelly

1½ quarts strawberry sherbet, softened

Whipped cream
Strawberry halves

Heat milk in heavy small saucepan until bubbles appear on surface. Remove from heat. Add butter and stir to melt. Cool milk completely.

Preheat oven to 400°F. Grease jelly roll pan. Line with parchment paper to within ½ inch of edge. Grease and flour paper, shaking off excess. Sift flour, baking powder and salt into small bowl. Using electric mixer, beat eggs and sugar until slowly dissolving ribbon forms when beaters are lifted. Gently fold in flour. Gently fold in milk mixture and vanilla. Spread batter in prepared pan. Bake until cake is pale golden, about 12 to 15 minutes.

Set kitchen towel on work surface. Dust generously with powdered sugar. Turn cake out onto prepared towel. Remove paper. Trim crisp edges from cake. Using towel as aid, roll cake up jelly roll fashion. Cool completely; do not remove kitchen towel.

Unroll cake. Using moistened metal spatula, spread with jelly. Reroll cake jelly roll fashion. Freeze 1 hour.

Line 9x5-inch loaf pan with plastic wrap, allowing overhang. Cut jelly roll into ¼-inch slices. Line bottom and sides of pan with slices. Fill with sherbet, spreading evenly. Cover with plastic. Freeze several hours or overnight.

Wrap hot towel around pan. Unmold loaf onto platter. Spoon whipped cream into pastry bag fitted with star tip. Pipe rosettes down center of loaf. Set strawberry half in center of each rosette. Serve immediately.

Hazelnut and Caramel Ice Cream Cake

10 servings

Amaretti-Hazelnut Crust
1¾ cups amaretti (Italian macaroons)
⅓ cup hazelnuts, toasted, husked and finely chopped
2 tablespoons (¼ stick) unsalted butter, melted and cooled

3 pints caramel, caramel fudge or praline ice cream

Caramel Sauce
1¼ cups sugar
¾ cup water

1 cup whipping cream

Hazelnut Whipped Cream
1 cup whipping cream, well chilled
2 tablespoons hazelnut liqueur
2 teaspoons sugar
2 nectarines, thinly sliced
Toasted hazelnuts

For crust: Oil bottom of 9-inch springform pan. Grind cookies in processor to fine crumbs. Measure ⅔ cup; transfer to bowl. Add hazelnuts. Mix in butter with fork. Press mixture evenly into bottom of pan. Freeze crust until firm, about 20 minutes.

Soften ice cream in refrigerator until spreadable. Spoon into prepared crust and smooth surface. Freeze until firm, at least 8 hours or overnight.

For sauce: Heat sugar and water in heavy medium saucepan over low heat, swirling pan occasionally, until sugar dissolves. Increase heat and boil, without stirring, until light brown.

Meanwhile, bring cream to simmer in heavy small saucepan. Reduce heat to low to keep warm. Reduce heat under syrup to low and cook until color of maple syrup, about 4 minutes. Carefully and gradually add hot cream (sauce will bubble). When bubbling stops, mix well. Place saucepan in shallow pan of water over low heat to keep warm. *(Can be prepared 2 days ahead. Cover and refrigerate. Reheat over very low heat, stirring constantly.)*

Place cake on platter. Run knife around edge of pan; remove sides. Refrigerate while preparing cream.

For whipped cream: Whip cream with liqueur and sugar until peaks form. Smooth over top and sides of cake. Arrange nectarine slices in ring atop cake. Place hazelnuts in center. Serve immediately. Pass warm sauce separately.

Macadamia Nut Mocha Meringue Frozen Cake

12 servings

1½ cups sugar
5 tablespoons sifted powdered sugar
7 egg whites, room temperature

2 pints coffee ice cream, softened
1 cup chopped unsalted macadamia nuts

2 pints chocolate chip ice cream, softened

2 cups whipping cream

Preheat oven to 150°F. Grease baking sheets; dust lightly with flour. Trace four 12-inch circles on sheets. Combine sugar and 4 tablespoons powdered sugar. Using electric mixer, beat whites until soft peaks form. Gradually add sugar mixture and beat until stiff and shiny. Spoon into pastry bag fitted with plain tip. Starting in center of each circle, pipe 1-inch-thick layer of meringue in spiral pattern. Transfer sheets to oven. Bake 2 hours. Turn off oven and let cooked meringues stand until light in color and dry to touch, about 5 hours.

Trim 3 meringue rounds to fit 12-inch springform pan. Set 1 round in bottom of pan. Spread with coffee ice cream. Sprinkle with ¼ cup nuts. Top with second meringue. Spread with chocolate chip ice cream. Sprinkle with ¼ cup nuts. Top with third meringue. Freeze until firm.

Coarsely chop fourth meringue round. Beat cream to stiff peaks. Combine remaining ½ cup nuts with remaining 1 tablespoon powdered sugar. Remove springform. Frost top and sides of cake with whipped cream. Press chopped meringue onto sides. Sprinkle nut mixture on top. Freeze until firm. Let soften 30 minutes in refrigerator before serving.

Bûche Glacé

For this dessert, frozen parfait is molded into the traditional bûche de Noël, or Yule log, and topped with lightly browned meringue.

8 to 10 servings

Parfait
1 cup milk
5 egg yolks
½ cup sugar
9 ounces bittersweet (not unsweetened) or semisweet chocolate, finely chopped
1½ ounces unsweetened chocolate, finely chopped
1½ teaspoons vanilla

1½ cups well-chilled whipping cream

Meringue
5 egg whites, room temperature
¼ teaspoon cream of tartar
1 cup sugar

¼ cup powdered sugar
Holly leaves or pine sprigs
Crème de Menthe Cream Sauce*

For parfait: Remove top and bottom from two 1-pound vegetable or fruit cans. Remove top from another 1-pound can; reserve top. Tape all 3 cans together, forming cylinder with can bottom at one end. Scald milk in heavy nonaluminum saucepan. Whisk yolks in medium bowl to blend. Gradually add sugar, whisking until pale and creamy. Gradually whisk in hot milk. Return mixture to saucepan. Stir over medium-low heat until custard thickens and coats spoon lightly (165°F to 170°F), about 8 minutes; do not boil. Strain into large bowl. Add bittersweet and unsweetened chocolate and vanilla and stir until chocolate melts. Cool completely.

Whip cream until soft peaks form. Fold into chocolate mixture. Spoon into mold. Push reserved can top tightly against parfait to eliminate air pockets. Cover and freeze overnight.

Cover 18x6-inch piece of cardboard completely with foil. Using can opener, remove bottom from mold. Wrap mold in hot towel. Push firmly on can top to run parfait onto foil-wrapped cardboard. Cut diagonal slice from each end of parfait. Press slices against parfait, one on each side, to resemble stumps of branches on log. Return parfait to freezer.

For meringue: Beat whites with cream of tartar in large bowl until soft peaks form. Add 1 cup sugar 1 tablespoon at a time, beating until stiff and glossy.

Spread meringue over parfait, covering completely and sealing meringue to foil. Using fork, texture meringue to resemble tree bark. Using knife, draw spiral pattern on stump ends. Return dessert to freezer to firm. *(Can be prepared 1 day ahead.)*

Just before serving, preheat oven to 475°F. Sift powdered sugar over dessert. Bake just until meringue is golden brown, watching carefully, 3 to 5 minutes. Garnish with holly leaves. Serve immediately, passing sauce separately.

*Crème de Menthe Cream Sauce

Makes about 2 cups

1 cup well-chilled whipping cream
2 tablespoons green or clear crème de menthe liqueur

1½ tablespoons sugar

Whip cream until just beginning to thicken. Mix in liqueur and sugar.

Frozen Fudge Cake with Brandied Cream

12 servings

10 eggs, separated
1 tablespoon distilled white vinegar
1 tablespoon water
1¾ cups sugar
10 ounces semisweet chocolate, broken into pieces
4½ teaspoons baking powder
¼ teaspoon salt
¾ cup (1½ sticks) unsalted butter, cut into 6 pieces, room temperature
4½ teaspoons vanilla

Brandied Cream
2¼ cups well-chilled whipping cream
3 tablespoons brandy
3 tablespoons sugar

Chocolate Glaze*

Position rack in center of oven and preheat to 350°F. Butter three 9-inch round cake pans. Line bottoms with parchment; butter paper.

Blend whites in processor 8 seconds. With machine running, pour vinegar and water through feed tube and process until whites hold shape in work bowl, about 2 minutes. Using spatula, gently transfer to large bowl. Wipe work bowl and blades dry with paper towels. Combine sugar, chocolate, baking powder and salt in work bowl and chop using 6 to 8 on/off turns, then process continuously until chocolate is as fine as sugar, stopping once to scrape down sides of work bowl, about 1 minute. Add butter and blend 30 seconds. Add yolks and vanilla and mix 10 seconds. Add ¼ of whites and process until well blended. Run spatula around inside of work bowl to loosen mixture. Spoon remaining whites atop batter. (Batter can also be added to remaining ¾ whites in bowl and folded to blend.) Mix using 3 on/off turns. Run spatula around inside of work bowl. Mix just until butter and whites are combined, using 3 or 4 on/off turns.

Divide batter among prepared pans. Bake until tester inserted in centers comes out clean, 32 to 35 minutes. Cool in pans 10 minutes. Run knife around cakes to loosen. Invert onto racks; discard parchment. Cool completely; cakes will sink in center. *(Can be prepared ahead. Wrap tightly and refrigerate 5 days or freeze 1 month.)*

Irwin Horowitz

From top to bottom: Hazelnut and
Caramel Ice Cream Cake; Chocolate-
Raisin Ice Cream Cake; Peach-Pecan
Ice Cream Cake; Queen of Sheba
Ice Cream Cake

Chocolate Pecan Torte with Strawberry Buttercream

Jerry Friedman

Clockwise from top: Turkish Coffee Torte; Austrian Hazelnut Cake; Deluxe Danish Apple Cake; Gateau St. James

Irwin Horowitz

Chocolate Chip and Currant Pound Cake

For cream: With machine running, pour cream through feed tube and process until thick, about 2 minutes. Scrape down sides of work bowl. Add brandy and sugar and process until sugar dissolves and cream is very thick, about 15 seconds.

Trim edges of cakes to even. Invert one layer onto platter. Spread cake with half of cream. Top with another cake layer and spread with remaining cream. Invert last cake layer over cream. Run spatula around sides to smooth. Freeze cake until solid.

Transfer cake to rack. Pour room-temperature Chocolate Glaze over frozen cake, letting some drip down sides. Using metal spatula, immediately smooth sides. Return cake to platter. *(Can be prepared 4 days ahead and frozen.)* Let cake soften slightly at room temperature before serving. (Can also be served at room temperature.)

*Chocolate Glaze

Makes about 2 cups

9 tablespoons water
6 tablespoons (¾ stick) unsalted butter
3 tablespoons safflower oil

3 ounces semisweet chocolate, broken into pieces

9 tablespoons sugar
6 tablespoons unsweetened cocoa powder
Pinch of salt
2 tablespoons brandy

Combine water, butter and oil in saucepan and bring to boil.

Chop chocolate in processor with sugar, cocoa and salt using 6 to 8 on/off turns, then process continuously until chocolate is as fine as sugar. With machine running, pour hot butter mixture through feed tube and process until chocolate is melted, stopping once to scrape down sides of work bowl. Add brandy and blend 3 seconds. Cool to room temperature.

Chocolate Chip-Coffee Ice Cream Cake

There will be leftover cookies to serve with this elegant ice cream cake.

8 to 10 servings

Chocolate Chip Cookies
1 cup all purpose flour
½ teaspoon salt
½ teaspoon baking soda
½ cup (1 stick) unsalted butter, room temperature
½ cup firmly packed light brown sugar
¼ cup sugar
1 egg

½ teaspoon vanilla
1 cup walnuts, coarsely chopped
¾ cup semisweet chocolate chips

½ cup coffee bean candies*
2 pints coffee ice cream

1 cup whipping cream, well chilled
1 tablespoon sugar
1 teaspoon coffee extract or 2 tablespoons coffee liqueur

For cookies: Preheat oven to 350°F. Butter baking sheets. Sift flour, salt and baking soda. Cream butter using electric mixer. Beat in sugars until smooth. Beat in egg and vanilla. Stir in flour mixture, then nuts and chocolate chips. Drop dough onto prepared sheets, using 1½ teaspoons for each cookie and spacing 2 inches apart. Flatten with back of fork dipped in water. Bake until cookies are light brown, about 7 minutes. Cool completely on racks. *(Cookies can be prepared up to 1 week ahead. Store in airtight container.)*

Reserve 21 coffee beans; coarsely chop remainder. Soften ice cream in refrigerator until spreadable.

Oil 8x4-inch loaf pan lined with aluminum foil. Cover pan bottom with 1 layer of cookies, flat sides down, fitting together tightly. Cover with half of ice cream, pressing firmly with back of spoon. Sprinkle with chopped coffee beans. Crumble 4 cookies and sprinkle over top. Add remaining ice cream, pressing firmly. Smooth top with spatula. Top with layer of 8 cookies, flat sides up, fitting together tightly. Cover and freeze at least 1 day.

Just before serving, run knife around edge of dessert. Invert onto platter. Refrigerate while preparing cream. Whip cream with 1 tablespoon sugar and coffee extract until stiff peaks form. Smooth ¾ of cream over sides of cake. Spoon remainder into pastry bag fitted with medium star tip. Pipe rosettes over top of cake. Decorate top with reserved coffee beans. Freeze 5 minutes.

*Available at specialty foods or candy stores.

Raspberry-Brownie Ice Cream Cake

8 to 10 servings

Fudge Brownies
- 2 ounces semisweet chocolate, chopped
- 3 tablespoons unsalted butter
- 4 tablespoons plus 2 teaspoons all purpose flour
- ¼ teaspoon baking powder
- Pinch of salt
- 1 egg, room temperature
- ½ cup sugar
- ½ teaspoon vanilla
- ⅓ cup walnuts, coarsely chopped

- 1 pint raspberry sherbet
- 2½ cups vanilla ice cream

Topping
- 1 cup whipping cream, well chilled
- 2 teaspoons sugar
- 1 teaspoon vanilla
- Fresh raspberries

For brownies: Position rack in center of oven and preheat to 350°F. Line 8-inch square pan with parchment or foil; butter paper or foil. Melt chocolate and 3 tablespoons butter in double boiler over hot, but not boiling, water. Stir until smooth. Cool slightly. Sift flour, baking powder and salt. Blend egg and sugar using electric mixer. Mix in vanilla. Gradually beat in chocolate mixture. Stir in dry ingredients, then walnuts, using wooden spoon. Spread batter evenly in prepared pan. Bake until tester inserted in center comes out dry, about 19 minutes. Cool completely in pan on rack. Invert onto rack and remove paper. Cut into 16 squares. Freeze brownies until firm but not solid, about 2 hours.

Line bottom of 8-inch square pan with waxed paper. Freeze about 15 minutes. Soften sherbet in refrigerator until spreadable. Smooth into prepared pan. Freeze until firm, about 15 minutes. Soften 1 cup ice cream in refrigerator until spreadable. Smooth over sherbet. Freeze until firm.

Cut each of the brownies into 2 layers. Cover ice cream with half of brownies, arranging around sides first, then filling in center. Press into ice cream. Freeze until firm, about 15 minutes.

Soften remaining 1½ cups ice cream in refrigerator. Spread over brownies. Freeze 15 minutes. Cover ice cream with remaining brownies, smooth sides up, arranging around sides first, then filling in center. Press into ice cream to even top. Cover and freeze for 8 hours or overnight.

Run knife around edges of dessert and invert onto platter; peel off parchment paper. Return to freezer.

For topping: Whip cream with sugar and vanilla until peaks form. Spoon into pastry bag fitted with medium star tip. Pipe mixture in ruffles over sides of cake. Pipe rosettes on top. Place raspberry atop each rosette. Serve with additional berries.

Queen of Sheba Ice Cream Cake

This dark chocolate cake is a wonderful do-ahead dessert.

10 to 12 servings

Cocoa-Almond Cake
½ cup blanched almonds, toasted
8 tablespoons sugar
¼ cup all purpose flour
2 tablespoons unsweetened cocoa powder
½ teaspoon baking powder
3 eggs, separated, room temperature
   Pinch of cream of tartar
¼ cup (½ stick) unsalted butter, melted and cooled

Chocolate Parfait
6 ounces semisweet chocolate, coarsely chopped
½ cup milk
4 egg yolks, room temperature
⅔ cup sugar

1 cup whipping cream, well chilled

¼ cup amaretto liqueur
2 tablespoons water

Chocolate Whipped Cream
1 ounce semisweet chocolate, coarsely chopped
½ cup whipping cream, well chilled
2 teaspoons sugar
½ teaspoon vanilla
7 whole blanched almonds

For cake: Position rack in center of oven and preheat to 350°F. Cover base of 9-inch springform pan with foil, then attach sides. Butter and flour foil and pan sides. Finely grind almonds with 2 tablespoons sugar in processor. Sift flour, cocoa and baking powder into small bowl. Stir in almond mixture. Beat yolks and 4 tablespoons sugar using electric mixer until slowly dissolving ribbon forms when beaters are lifted, about 5 minutes. Beat whites with cream of tartar in another bowl until stiff but not dry. Gradually add remaining 2 tablespoons sugar and beat until whites are stiff and shiny. Fold ⅓ of almond-cocoa mixture into yolks, then ⅓ of whites. Repeat twice, folding in butter just before final ⅓ of whites is incorporated.

Spoon batter into prepared pan, smoothing surface with spatula. Bake until tester inserted into center of cake comes out dry, about 20 minutes. Cool in pan on rack 5 minutes. Invert onto rack and cool completely.

For parfait: Melt chocolate in top of double boiler over hot, but not boiling, water. Bring milk to simmer in heavy medium saucepan over low heat. Whisk yolks and sugar in bowl until smooth. Gradually whisk in hot milk; return to saucepan. Stir over low heat until mixture leaves path on back of spoon when finger is drawn across, about 5 minutes; *do not boil.* Gradually whisk custard into chocolate until smooth. Cool completely, stirring occasionally.

Whip cream to soft peaks. Fold in chocolate mixture in 3 batches.

To assemble: Cut cake into 2 layers, using serrated knife. Set bottom layer cut side up in 9-inch springform pan. Combine liqueur and 2 tablespoons water. Brush 3 tablespoons onto cake in pan. Spoon half of chocolate parfait over, spreading to edge of cake. Top with second layer, cut side up. Brush with remaining liqueur. Spread with remaining parfait. Cover and freeze until firm, at least 4 hours.

Remove pan sides. Refrigerate cake while preparing cream.

For whipped cream: Melt chocolate in double boiler over hot, but not boiling, water. Stir until smooth. Remove from over water. Whip cream with sugar and vanilla to stiff peaks. Whisk in chocolate. Spoon mixture into pastry bag fitted with medium star tip. Set cake on platter. Pipe 12 rosettes of chocolate cream around top edge of cake and pipe 1 large rosette in center. Set almond on alternate rosettes and in center of cake. Serve immediately.

Black Forest Ice Cream Torte

*Assemble this variation on a
classic cake at least one day
before serving. The vanilla ice
cream is superb, but a good-
quality one from the grocery
store can be used to save time.*

12 servings

Brandied Bing Cherries
 1 **16-ounce can pitted Bing cherries
   in heavy syrup, drained (½ cup
   syrup reserved)**
 2 **tablespoons sugar**
 3 **tablespoons kirsch**

Chocolate Biscuit
 3 **egg yolks, room temperature**
 1 **egg**
 ⅓ **cup sugar**
 1 **tablespoon water**
 ½ **teaspoon vanilla**
 2 **tablespoons cake flour**
 2 **tablespoons cornstarch**
 2 **tablespoons unsweetened cocoa
   powder (preferably Dutch process)**
 2 **egg whites, room temperature**
 ⅛ **teaspoon cream of tartar**

   Pinch of salt
 1 **tablespoon sugar**

Vanilla Ice Cream
1½ **cups half and half**
 7 **tablespoons sugar**
 1 **vanilla bean, split**
 9 **egg yolks, room temperature**
 ½ **cup sugar**
1½ **cups whipping cream**
 1 **teaspoon vanilla extract**

 2 **tablespoons kirsch**

   Ice cubes

   Ganache Glaze*

 ½ **cup well-chilled whipping cream**
 1 **tablespoon sugar**

For cherries: Set 12 cherries aside for garnish; cut remainder in half. Cook ½ cup reserved cherry syrup and sugar in heavy medium saucepan over low heat, swirling pan occasionally, until sugar dissolves. Increase heat and bring to boil. Add all cherries, cover and simmer 1 minute. Transfer cherries to glass jar, using slotted spoon. Add kirsch to cherries. Boil syrup until reduced to ¼ cup. Pour over cherries. Cover jar tightly and tilt several times to mix through. Refrigerate at least 12 hours. *(Can be prepared 3 months ahead.)*

For biscuit: Preheat oven to 450°F. Grease two 9-inch round cake pans. Line with parchment; grease paper. Dust with flour. Using electric mixer, beat yolks, whole egg and ⅓ cup sugar until tripled in volume. Beat in water and vanilla. Sift together flour, cornstarch and cocoa. Then resift onto eggs. Using whisk, fold together thoroughly. Beat whites, cream of tartar and salt in another bowl until soft peaks form. Add 1 tablespoon sugar and beat until almost stiff but not dry. Gently fold ¼ of whites into batter, then fold in remaining whites. Divide batter between prepared pans, tilting pans back and forth to level. Bake until tester inserted in center comes out clean, about 7 minutes. Invert cakes onto parchment or waxed paper and cool completely. *(Can be prepared ahead. Wrap tightly in plastic and store at room temperature 1 day or freeze up to 5 days.)*

For ice cream: Heat half and half, 7 tablespoons sugar and vanilla bean in heavy medium saucepan over low heat, swirling pan occasionally, until sugar dissolves. Increase heat and bring to boil. In small bowl whisk yolks and ½ cup sugar to blend. Whisk in ⅓ cup of hot half and half, then whisk yolks into remaining half and half. Stir over medium heat until thermometer registers 175°F and mixture thickens slightly. Immediately strain through fine sieve. Scrape seeds from vanilla bean into mixture. Add 1½ cups whipping cream and vanilla extract. Refrigerate until well chilled.

Transfer mixture to ice cream maker. Process according to manufacturer's instructions, adding kirsch when almost frozen. *(Can be prepared 2 hours ahead and frozen. If frozen solid, soften slightly in refrigerator before continuing.)*

To assemble: Drain cherries, reserving syrup. Pat cherries dry with paper towels. Set 12 whole cherries aside for garnish. Brush cherry syrup onto all surfaces of cake. Place one cake layer on bottom of 9-inch springform pan; attach sides. Place springform in larger pan and surround with ice (to prevent ice cream from melting). Spread half of ice cream onto cake layer. Top with half of cherries, pressing in slightly and arranging a few with cut sides against pan sides. Repeat with remaining ice cream and then remaining halved cherries. Press second cake layer firmly on top. Cover torte with foil. Remove springform from larger pan and freeze torte at least 24 hours. *(Can be prepared 2 days ahead.)*

Pour tepid Ganache Glaze onto center of torte. Working quickly, tilt pan to spread glaze over entire surface. *(Can be prepared 4 hours ahead and frozen.)*

Wipe sides of torte pan once with warm, damp towel. Remove pan sides. Refrigerate torte 1 hour to soften. Just before serving, beat ½ cup whipping cream and 1 tablespoon sugar until firm peaks form. Spoon into pastry bag fitted with star tip. Pipe whipped cream in rosettes atop cake. Top with reserved whole cherries.

*Ganache Glaze

Makes about ⅔ cup

3 ounces semisweet chocolate (preferably imported), finely chopped	⅓ cup whipping cream, scalded 2 teaspoons Cognac

Place chocolate in small bowl. Add hot cream. Cover and let stand 5 minutes. Add Cognac and stir slowly until chocolate melts and mixture is smooth; *do not incorporate air bubbles.* Let cool just until tepid (small amount of glaze spooned onto surface of glaze will be absorbed). *(Can be prepared 10 days ahead. Reheat Ganache Glaze in top of double boiler over barely simmering water until tepid, stirring constantly.)*

Chocolate-Raisin Ice Cream Cake

A great combination: rum-raisin ice cream and chocolate meringue.

10 to 12 servings

Cocoa Meringue
¾ cup plus 3 tablespoons powdered sugar
5 tablespoons unsweetened cocoa powder
5 egg whites, room temperature
¼ teaspoon cream of tartar

10 tablespoons sugar

3 pints rum-raisin ice cream

½ cup whipping cream, well chilled
1 teaspoon sugar

For meringue: Position 1 rack in center of oven and another in lower third; preheat to 180°F (or lowest setting). Grease corners of 2 baking sheets and line with foil or parchment. Butter foil or paper and dust with flour. Using 9-inch springform pan as guide, trace circle on each sheet. Fit pastry bag with ½-inch plain tip. Sift powdered sugar with cocoa. Beat whites with cream of tartar with electric mixer at medium speed until soft peaks form. Add 10 tablespoons sugar 1 tablespoon at a time and beat until meringue is shiny. Gently fold in cocoa mixture.

Spoon meringue into prepared pastry bag. Pipe out meringue ¾ inch thick onto 1 circle on baking sheet, beginning at center and spiraling outward until circle is completely covered. Repeat with second circle. Replace pastry bag tip with medium star tip. Pipe remaining meringue onto empty portions of baking sheets into mounds ½ inch in diameter and 1 inch high with pointed tops, forming "kisses." Bake until kisses are firm and dry, about 1 to 1½ hours (depending on temperature of oven). To test, remove 1 kiss and cool 2 minutes. Break apart; it should be dry and not sticky.

Transfer kisses to rack. Continue baking layers until firm and dry, about 1½ hours. Gently release from paper, using large metal spatula. If bottom of meringue is sticky, return to pan and bake until dry. Remove from paper and cool on rack. *(Can be prepared 1 week ahead. Store in airtight container.)*

Soften ice cream in refrigerator until spreadable. Carefully trim meringue layers to fit 9-inch springform pan. Set 1 layer in pan. Spread with half of ice cream. Set second layer on top. Spread with remaining ice cream. Freeze at least 8 hours.

Just before serving, whip cream with 1 teaspoon sugar until soft peaks form. Set cake on platter. Run knife around edge of pan; release sides. Smooth whipped cream in thin layer over top and sides of cake, using metal spatula. Decorate top with meringue kisses.

Frozen Chocolate Mousse Cake with Candied Fruit and Chartreuse

A magnificent do-ahead dessert. Use a stencil with a holiday motif to decorate the top with powdered sugar.

12 to 16 servings

1 cup ¼-inch dice candied fruit (do not use cherries)
½ cup green Chartreuse liqueur

Meringue
5 egg whites, room temperature
Pinch of salt
Pinch of cream of tartar
8 tablespoons sugar
1½ cups ground toasted blanched almonds

Mousse
2 cups whipping cream
8 egg yolks, room temperature

½ cup sugar
1 teaspoon vanilla
Pinch of salt
9 ounces Swiss bittersweet or semisweet chocolate, melted and cooled to room temperature
4 egg whites, room temperature

Unsweetened cocoa powder
Powdered sugar
Holly sprigs (optional)

Soak 1 cup diced candied fruit in Chartreuse liqueur overnight.

Line bottom of 9x13x2-inch straight-sided pan with waxed paper. Line sides of pan with strips of waxed paper.

For meringue: Preheat oven to 325°F. Butter and flour 2 baking sheets. Trace 9x13-inch rectangle on each, using bottom of waxed paper-lined pan as guide. Using electric mixer, beat whites, salt and cream of tartar until soft peaks form. Add 2 tablespoons sugar and beat until stiff but not dry. Fold in remaining 6 tablespoons sugar and almonds. Spread meringue evenly over rectangles. Bake until golden brown and dry, 20 to 30 minutes. Loosen meringues from sheets, but leave in place. Cool on racks. *(Can be prepared 1 day ahead. Wrap airtight. Recrisp in 250°F oven for about 10 minutes before continuing if necessary.)*

Trim meringues to fit waxed paper-lined pan. Place most attractive one smooth side down in pan.

For mousse: Beat cream until soft peaks form. Drain 3 tablespoons of Chartreuse from fruit. Add to cream and beat until soft peaks form again. Refrigerate. Using electric mixer, beat yolks, sugar, vanilla and salt until pale yellow and slowly dissolving ribbon forms when beater is lifted. Beat in chocolate. Fold in candied fruit with any remaining Chartreuse. Using clean, dry beaters, beat whites until stiff but not dry. Gently fold ¼ of whites into chocolate mixture, then fold in remaining whites. Fold whipped cream into mousse. Pour into meringue-lined pan. Top with second meringue, smooth side up. Freeze overnight. *(Can be prepared 2 days ahead.)*

Invert dessert onto platter. Remove waxed paper. Let stand at room temperature 15 minutes. Slide strips of waxed paper under dessert. Dust top with cocoa. Place decorative stencil atop cocoa and dust with powdered sugar. Remove stencil and paper strips. Garnish platter with holly. To serve, cut dessert with serrated knife.

4 ❦ Flourless and Nut Cakes

Many people call these tortes, from the German word for cakes. Because many European cakes are made primarily with ground nuts or bread crumbs instead of flour, a torte is often defined as a cake without flour.

Nut cakes have a rich, dense texture and will stay fresh for days. Made with little or no butter, they are a delicate balance of crunchy, finely ground nuts and well-beaten separated eggs. They can be served plain, with just a dusting of powdered sugar, or fancy, with the addition of fillings and frostings. Try Lemon Almond Cake (page 73) or Gâteau Saint James (page 77), simply decorated with a pattern of the English rising sun. The sky's the limit with desserts like Ginger-Almond Gâteau with Fresh Strawberries (page 75), Spanish Cream Torte (page 76), a good do-ahead dessert, and California Harvest Torte (page 77), covered with chocolate glaze and garnished with caramelized apricots.

Some of our flourless cakes, such as Deluxe Danish Apple Cake (page 64), call for cake crumbs instead of nuts. A combination of nuts and crumbs gives an interesting texture to Marzipan Carrot Cake (page 66). A few, such as the incredibly rich Chocolate Truffle Cake (page 72) and Peanut Butter Meringue Cake (page 69), use neither nuts nor crumbs.

❧ *Flourless Cakes*

Deluxe Danish Apple Cake

8 to 10 servings

6 pounds Golden Delicious or pippin apples
1 cup sugar
2 cups water
3 tablespoons fresh lemon juice

6 tablespoons (¾ stick) unsalted butter
3 cups dry pound cake crumbs
4 ounces apple jelly
½ cup crumbled almond macaroons

Caramelized Almonds
1¼ cups sliced almonds (4 ounces)
1 tablespoon sugar

Marzipan
8 ounces almond paste
1 cup (or more) powdered sugar
1 tablespoon egg white
½ teaspoon almond extract

1½ cups whipping cream

Peel, halve and core apples; cut into ¼-inch slices. (If using pippins, immediately drop slices into acidulated water to prevent discoloring; Golden Delicious apples do not brown as quickly.)

Combine sugar, water and lemon juice in large pan and bring to boil, stirring just until sugar is dissolved. Add about ¼ of apples and poach until tender but not mushy, about 5 to 7 minutes. Remove apples using slotted spoon and let drain on paper towels. Repeat this procedure with remaining apples.

Preheat oven to 400°F. Melt butter in medium saucepan over low heat. Add cake crumbs and toss until all butter is absorbed. Sprinkle 1½ cups in bottom of 9-inch springform pan; press to form crust. Add half the apples, spreading evenly. Dot with all of jelly. Top with 1 cup cake crumbs and all of macaroons; press lightly to make cake compact. Top with remaining apples and cover with crumbs; press down again.

Set pan on foil-lined baking sheet. Bake until top is golden and apples are tender, 45 to 60 minutes. If top begins to brown too quickly, cover loosely with foil. Remove cake from oven and let stand until cool. Place piece of foil over top, then set flat plate directly on foil. Place 2-pound weight on plate for several hours or overnight.

For almonds: Preheat oven to 350°F. Spread almonds on jelly roll pan. Sprinkle with sugar. Toast until almonds are golden brown, stirring and shaking pan several times. Let cool completely.

For marzipan: Combine ingredients in processor and mix until smooth and pliable. Sprinkle work surface with powdered sugar. Knead marzipan until consistency of pie dough, adding more sugar if needed. Cover with plastic to keep from drying out.

To assemble: Unmold cake by running thin knife around edges; remove sides but leave cake on metal base. Sprinkle surface lightly with powdered sugar and roll marzipan into 15-inch circle. Drape over cake, pressing gently against top and sides to enclose completely.

Whip cream until stiff. Spread about ⅔ over entire cake; cover top and sides with almonds. Use remaining ⅓ of whipped cream to make rosettes around edge. Refrigerate until ready to serve.

❧

Banana Nutmeg Cake with Caramelized Brown Sugar Sauce

10 to 12 servings

5 eggs, separated, room temperature
1 cup sugar
3 small ripe bananas, mashed (about 1 cup)
⅓ cup vegetable oil
2 teaspoons grated lemon peel

1 teaspoon grated orange peel
¼ teaspoon salt
¾ cup matzo cake meal
¼ cup potato starch
½ teaspoon freshly grated nutmeg
Caramelized Brown Sugar Sauce*

Preheat oven to 325°F. Using electric mixer, beat yolks and ½ cup sugar in large bowl until slowly dissolving ribbon forms when beaters are lifted, about 5 minutes. Blend in bananas, oil and peels. Using clean, dry beaters, beat whites with salt in large bowl until soft peaks form. Gradually add remaining ½ cup sugar and beat until stiff but not dry. Fold in yolk mixture. Sift together cake meal, potato starch and nutmeg. Gently fold into egg mixture in two additions. Turn into greased 10-inch bundt pan, smoothing top. Bake until tester inserted in center comes out clean, about 1 hour. Invert onto rack and cool. Cut into thin slices. Spoon sauce over and serve.

*Caramelized Brown Sugar Sauce

Makes about 1 cup

¾ cup firmly packed dark brown sugar
6 tablespoons water
2 teaspoons finely grated lemon peel

¼ teaspoon salt
2 small ripe bananas, halved lengthwise and thinly sliced
4 teaspoons fresh lemon juice

Combine sugar, water, peel and salt in heavy medium saucepan and bring to boil. Reduce heat to low. Add bananas and simmer gently 5 minutes. Remove from heat. Stir in lemon juice. Press through sieve. Serve warm or cold.

Carrot Almond Cake

8 to 10 servings

Matzo cake meal (for pan)
4 eggs, separated, room temperature
½ cup firmly packed light brown sugar
1½ cups carrots, finely grated
1 teaspoon vanilla (optional)

¼ teaspoon salt
½ cup sugar

1 cup finely ground toasted almonds
3 tablespoons matzo cake meal
½ teaspoon cinnamon

Preheat oven to 350°F. Grease bottom of 8-inch springform pan; dust with cake meal, shaking off excess. Using electric mixer, beat yolks and brown sugar in large bowl until slowly dissolving ribbon forms when beaters are lifted, about 5 minutes. Stir in carrots and vanilla. Using clean, dry beaters, beat whites with salt until soft peaks form. Gradually add sugar and beat until whites are stiff but not dry. Gently fold in yolk mixture.

Combine almonds, 3 tablespoons cake meal and cinnamon. Fold gently into egg mixture. Turn into prepared pan, smoothing top. Bake until tester inserted in center comes out clean, about 1 hour. Immediately run knife around edge. Cool completely in pan on rack. Remove springform before serving.

Marzipan Carrot Cake

A delicately spiced cake with a chocolate glaze.

12 servings

3 cups grated peeled carrots

1¾ cups hazelnuts, toasted, husked and ground

1 cup plus 2 tablespoons fresh sponge cake crumbs

4 teaspoons baking powder

1 tablespoon cinnamon

4½ teaspoons rum

2 teaspoons grated lemon peel

5 drops of vanilla

5 eggs, separated, room temperature

⅔ cup sugar

¼ cup hot water

¼ teaspoon cream of tartar

⅔ cup sugar

8 ounces marzipan

Chocolate Glaze

7 ounces bittersweet (not unsweetened) or semisweet chocolate, coarsely chopped

½ cup (1 stick) unsalted butter

1 tablespoon corn syrup

1 drop of green food coloring

3 drops of red food coloring

2 drops of yellow food coloring

Preheat oven to 325°F. Grease 3-inch-deep 9-inch-diameter cake pan. Line bottom with parchment; grease paper. Dust pan and paper with flour. Combine first 8 ingredients in large bowl. Using electric mixer, beat yolks, ⅔ cup sugar and hot water until pale yellow and slowly dissolving ribbon forms when beaters are lifted. Gently fold into carrot mixture. Using clean, dry beater, beat whites with cream of tartar until soft peaks form. Add ⅔ cup sugar 1 tablespoon at a time, beating until stiff and shiny. Gently fold ¼ of whites into batter; gently fold in remaining whites. Pour batter into pan. Bake until tester inserted in center comes out clean, about 1½ hours. Cool cake completely in pan on rack.

Invert cake, discarding paper. Arrange top side up on platter. Roll marzipan out between sheets of waxed paper to 12-inch-diameter round. Remove top sheet of paper and invert marzipan atop cake. Gently smooth onto cake. Discard paper. Trim edges of marzipan; reserve trimmings for garnish.

For glaze: Melt chocolate with butter and corn syrup in top of double boiler over barely simmering water, stirring until mixture is smooth.

Spread thin layer of glaze over torte, filling in any cracks in marzipan. Pour remaining glaze onto center of torte; smooth over top and sides, using metal spatula. *(Can be prepared 1 day ahead. Let stand at room temperature.)*

Mix green coloring into 2 teaspoons of reserved marzipan. Mix red and yellow coloring into remainder. Form orange marzipan into carrots. Press green marzipan through sieve to form carrot tops. Gently press into wide end of carrots. Just before serving, place carrots in center of cake.

Carrot Torte

The food processor makes quick work of shredding the carrots and coconut for this flavorful cake.

8 to 10 servings

1 medium coconut

6 eggs, separated

1¼ cups sugar

1 tablespoon distilled white vinegar

1½ cups pecans

2 medium carrots, peeled and cut into 1-inch pieces

2 slices firm white bread, quartered

1 teaspoon grated orange peel (orange part only)

1 tablespoon baking powder

1 teaspoon cinnamon

1 teaspoon ground ginger

¼ teaspoon ground mace

¼ teaspoon salt

½ cup (1 stick) unsalted butter, cut into 8 pieces, room temperature

2 tablespoons fresh orange juice

Cream Cheese Frosting*

Position rack in center of oven and preheat to 400°F. Pierce holes through coconut at 3 soft spots on 1 end using hammer and nail. Drain liquid and reserve for another use. Bake coconut 20 minutes. Wrap in towel. Sharply pound center of coconut with hammer to crack open. Separate meat from shell. Remove brown skin using vegetable peeler. Cut into 1½-inch squares. Reduce oven to 350°F.

Butter 9-inch springform pan. Line bottom with parchment; butter paper.

Blend whites and ¼ cup sugar in processor work bowl 8 seconds. With machine running, pour vinegar through feed tube and whip until whites hold shape, about 2 minutes, 20 seconds. Gently transfer whites to medium bowl. Do not clean work bowl. Finely chop 4 squares of coconut, pecans, carrots, bread and orange peel with remaining 1 cup sugar, baking powder, cinnamon, ginger, mace and salt, stopping twice to scrape down sides of work bowl. Add yolks and blend 30 seconds, stopping once to scrape down sides. Add butter and orange juice and mix 30 seconds. Spoon whites onto carrot mixture and blend, using 2 on/off turns. Run spatula around inside of work bowl to loosen mixture. Blend just until whites are incorporated, 1 or 2 on/off turns (some streaks of white should remain).

Spoon batter into prepared pan. Bake until toothpick inserted in center comes out clean, about 1 hour. Cool in pan on rack 10 minutes. Remove sides of pan and cool completely. *(Can be prepared ahead to this point. Wrap tightly and refrigerate up to 3 days or freeze up to 6 months. Bring torte back to room temperature before continuing.)*

Place 8 squares of coconut in processor feed tube and shred, using firm pressure. Set aside. (Reserve remaining coconut for another use.) Brush loose crumbs from torte. Spread thin layer of Cream Cheese Frosting on sides. Smooth remaining frosting over top, using long thin spatula. Press coconut into sides. Serve within 2 hours.

*Cream Cheese Frosting

Makes about 1½ cups

1 **8-ounce package cream cheese, quartered, room temperature**	½ **cup powdered sugar** 1 **tablespoon fresh orange juice**

Blend all ingredients in processor until smooth, stopping once to scrape down sides of work bowl, about 30 seconds. Use frosting immediately.

Raspberry Dacquoise Cake

To soften the meringue layer, assemble this elegant and colorful dessert at least three hours before serving.

10 to 12 servings

Meringue
  Matzo cake meal (for pan)
  3 **egg whites, room temperature**
  ¼ **teaspoon fresh lemon juice**
  Pinch of salt
  1 **teaspoon vanilla (optional)**
  ½ **cup plus 2 tablespoons sugar**
  ⅓ **cup finely ground blanched almonds**
  ¼ **cup potato starch**

Honey-Raspberry Cake
  6 **eggs, separated, room temperature**
  ⅔ **cup sugar**

  ⅓ **cup vegetable oil**
  ¼ **cup honey**
  ¼ **cup strained raspberry jam**
  1 **teaspoon vanilla (optional)**
  ¼ **teaspoon salt**
  ½ **cup matzo cake meal**
  ¼ **cup potato starch**

  2¼ **cups strained raspberry jam**
    Fresh raspberries (optional)

For meringue: Preheat oven to 325°F. Grease 2 baking sheets; dust lightly with cake meal. Draw 10-inch circle in center of 1 sheet and 8-inch circle in center of second.

Using electric mixer, beat whites, lemon juice and salt in large bowl until soft peaks form. Mix in vanilla. Add ½ cup sugar 1 tablespoon at a time and beat until stiff but not dry. Combine remaining 2 tablespoons sugar, almonds and potato starch and gently fold into whites. Cover 10-inch circle on prepared baking sheet with ½-inch-thick layer of meringue. Cover 8-inch circle on prepared sheet with remaining meringue. Bake until layers are dry and lightly colored, about 35 minutes. Transfer to racks and cool completely.

For cake: Preheat oven to 350°F. Using electric mixer, beat yolks and ⅓ cup sugar in large bowl until slowly dissolving ribbon forms when beaters are lifted, about 5 minutes. Gradually mix in oil, honey, ¼ cup jam and vanilla. Using clean, dry beaters, beat whites and salt until soft peaks form. Add remaining ⅓ cup sugar 1 tablespoon at a time and beat until stiff but not dry. Spoon ¼ of whites over yolk mixture; sift cake meal and potato starch over and gently fold together. Fold in remaining whites. Spread batter in ungreased 10-inch springform pan. Bake until cake is springy to touch, about 50 minutes, covering top with foil if cake browns too quickly. Immediately invert pan on rack. Cool cake in pan.

Run knife around edge of cake; remove springform. Using long serrated knife, split cake into two layers. Slide spatula under cake to release pan bottom. Transfer bottom layer to platter. Spread with ¾ cup jam. Top with 10-inch meringue layer, pressing very lightly. Trim meringue to even edges. Spread meringue with ¾ cup jam. Top with second cake layer. Crush 8-inch meringue layer to coarse crumbs, using processor or rolling pin. Spread remaining ¾ cup jam over top and sides of cake. Press meringue crumbs into sides and over top of cake. Let stand at least 3 hours to soften meringue layer. Garnish with raspberries.

Nina's Greek Nut Cake with Rum Syrup

10 servings

Cake
Fine dry breadcrumbs
½ cup (1 stick) unsalted butter, room temperature
1 cup sugar
5 eggs, separated, room temperature
¼ cup milk
3 tablespoons dark rum
1 teaspoon vanilla
1 teaspoon almond extract
1 6-ounce box zwieback, finely crushed
2 teaspoons baking powder

1 teaspoon baking soda
1 teaspoon cinnamon
¼ teaspoon ground cloves
1 cup coarsely chopped walnuts

Pinch of salt

Rum Syrup
1 small lemon, halved
⅔ cup sugar
½ cup water
1 cinnamon stick
3 tablespoons dark rum

For cake: Preheat oven to 350°F. Butter 9-inch square cake pan. Sprinkle lightly with breadcrumbs, shaking out excess. Using electric mixer, beat butter until softened. Gradually add sugar and beat until light and fluffy. Beat in yolks 1 at a time. Blend in milk, rum, vanilla and almond extract. Combine zwieback, baking powder, baking soda, cinnamon and cloves in separate bowl. Stir into rum mixture. Fold in chopped walnuts; do not overmix.

Using electric mixer with clean, dry beaters, beat whites with salt until stiff but not dry. Gently fold ¼ of whites into batter to loosen. Fold in remaining whites. Pour batter into prepared pan. Bake until tester inserted in center comes out clean, about 40 minutes. Cool cake in pan on rack.

For syrup: Squeeze juice from lemon (you should have 2 to 3 tablespoons); reserve lemon halves. Heat sugar and water in heavy small saucepan over low heat until sugar dissolves, swirling pan occasionally. Add lemon juice, lemon halves and cinnamon stick and boil until syrupy, about 5 minutes. Add rum and boil 30 seconds.

Using skewer or large fork, pierce surface of cake. Strain half of syrup over top. When absorbed, strain remaining syrup over. Cut cake into diamonds. Serve warm or at room temperature.

Peanut Brittle Meringue Cake

10 to 12 servings

8 egg whites, room temperature
2 cups sugar
1 tablespoon distilled white vinegar
1 tablespoon vanilla

2 cups whipping cream
2 cups crushed peanut brittle

Preheat oven to 300°F. Line two 6x9-inch baking pans* with waxed paper. Beat whites until foamy, using electric mixer. Sift sugar twice. Gradually beat into whites until stiff but not dry. Blend in vinegar and vanilla. Spread meringue into prepared pans. Bake 45 minutes. Turn oven off and let meringues stand in oven with door closed 25 minutes. Turn out onto rack and cool. *(Meringue layers can be prepared 1 day ahead. Store in airtight container at room temperature.)*

Whip cream until soft peaks form. Transfer 1 meringue layer to serving platter. Spread with half of cream. Sprinkle with half of peanut brittle. Top with second meringue layer, pressing gently. Frost top and sides of cake with remaining cream. Press remaining peanut brittle onto top and sides of cake. *(Cake can be assembled 2 hours ahead and refrigerated.)*

*If unavailable, two 7x10¾-inch baking pans can be substituted.

Macaroon Torte

8 to 12 servings

Coconut Cake
1½ cups finely shredded dried
    unsweetened coconut*

2 tablespoons cornstarch
4 eggs, separated, room temperature
    Pinch of cream of tartar
¾ cup sugar
1 teaspoon vanilla

Topping
2 kiwis, peeled and cut into ⅛-inch-
    thick slices

1 papaya, peeled, seeded and cut into
    ⅛-inch-thick slices
½ pineapple, peeled, cored, sliced ¼
    inch thick and cut into 1-inch
    squares
1½ cups whipping cream
3 tablespoons sugar
1 tablespoon dark rum

2 tablespoons dark rum
    Toasted flaked coconut

For cake: Preheat oven to 400°F. Sprinkle coconut on baking sheet. Bake just until dry, 1 to 4 minutes. Cool. Reduce oven temperature to 325°F.

Grease two 8-inch-diameter cake pans. Line with parchment; grease and flour paper. Combine coconut and cornstarch. Beat whites with cream of tartar until soft peaks form. Add ½ cup sugar 1 tablespoon at a time and beat until stiff but not dry.

Beat yolks with remaining ¼ cup sugar and vanilla until pale yellow and slowly dissolving ribbon forms when beaters are lifted. Fold ¼ of whites into yolks, then fold in remaining whites. Add coconut mixture and fold just until blended. Divide batter between prepared pans. Bake until cakes pull away from sides of pan, about 20 minutes. Invert onto towel-lined rack and cool completely; cakes will fall in center. *(Can be prepared 1 day ahead and refrigerated.)*

For topping: Drain fruit on paper towels. Whip cream with sugar and 1 tablespoon rum until peaks form.

Discard paper from cakes; gently press cakes to flatten. Place 1 layer on platter. Sprinkle with 1 tablespoon rum. Spread with some of whipped cream. Arrange half of fruit atop cream. Top with second layer; sprinkle with remaining 1 tablespoon rum. Trim sides of cake to even. Smooth remaining whipped cream over top and sides of cake. Arrange remaining fruit decoratively atop cake. Press toasted coconut into sides. *(Can be prepared 2 hours ahead and refrigerated.)*

*Also called macaroon coconut, available at natural foods stores.

Turkish Coffee Torte

8 to 10 servings

Layers
- 6 eggs, separated
- ½ teaspoon cream of tartar
- 1 cup sugar

- 1 tablespoon coffee liqueur
- ¾ cup sifted Turkish coffee powder
- ½ pound walnuts, ground

Chocolate-Mocha Buttercream
- 1 cup (2 sticks) unsalted butter, room temperature
- 8 ounces bittersweet chocolate, melted and cooled
- ½ cup powdered sugar

- 1 egg yolk
- 1 tablespoon brandy or coffee liqueur
- 1½ teaspoons instant coffee powder

- 4 tablespoons brandy or coffee liqueur
- ½ cup apricot or raspberry jam

Bittersweet Cocoa Glaze
- 1 cup plus 3 tablespoons sugar
- 1 cup unsweetened cocoa powder
- ⅔ cup evaporated milk
- ½ cup (1 stick) unsalted butter
- 1 teaspoon instant coffee powder

For layers: Preheat oven to 325°F. Butter bottoms of two 9-inch springform pans or line two 9-inch cake pans with parchment paper; set aside. Beat egg whites until foamy. Add cream of tartar and beat until soft peaks form. Gradually add ⅓ cup sugar and continue beating until whites are stiff but not dry.

Using same beater, whip egg yolks with remaining ⅔ cup sugar until thick and pale yellow. Blend in coffee liqueur. Combine coffee and ground walnuts. Fold into yolk mixture. Gradually fold in whites. Divide batter between prepared pans and bake until tester inserted in center comes out clean, 20 to 25 minutes. Cool completely.

For buttercream: Combine ingredients and beat until fluffy; set aside.

To assemble: Unmold cakes by running thin knife around edges; remove sides but leave cakes on metal bases. Brush each layer with 2 tablespoons brandy or liqueur. Spread top of one layer with jam; spread buttercream ¼ inch thick over second layer. Invert one layer over the other; carefully remove metal base or parchment paper from top. Spread most of remaining buttercream completely over cake; pipe rosettes from the rest onto waxed paper and chill. Set cake in freezer for at least 2 hours.

When ready to complete cake, prepare glaze. Combine ingredients in small saucepan. Place over low heat and cook, stirring constantly, until very smooth and slightly thickened, about 5 minutes. Let cool a few minutes.

Remove cake from freezer (if necessary remove parchment paper from bottom layer), and set on wire rack over waxed paper. Pour warm glaze over top of cake, smoothing quickly with knife to cover completely. Let cool. Set chilled butter cream rosettes on top when ready to serve.

Chocolate Mousse Hazelnut Cake

10 to 12 servings

Cake

Matzo cake meal (for pan)
1 cup hazelnuts (3 ounces), toasted and ground
½ cup matzo cake meal
2 tablespoons potato starch
¼ teaspoon cinnamon
8 egg yolks, room temperature
½ cup sugar
2 teaspoons vanilla (optional)
4 egg whites, room temperature

⅛ teaspoon salt
⅓ cup sugar

Mousse

8 ounces semisweet chocolate
¼ cup strong freshly brewed coffee

4 eggs, separated, room temperature
1 tablespoon brandy (or rum)
2 tablespoons sugar

Shaved semisweet chocolate

For cake: Preheat oven to 400°F. Grease bottom of 10-inch springform pan. Dust with cake meal, shaking off excess. Combine hazelnuts, ½ cup cake meal, potato starch and cinnamon in small bowl. Using electric mixer, beat yolks and ½ cup sugar until slowly dissolving ribbon forms when beaters are lifted. Blend in vanilla if desired. Using clean, dry beaters, beat whites and salt in another bowl until soft peaks form. Gradually add ⅓ cup sugar and beat until stiff but not dry. Gently fold ⅓ of whites into yolk mixture to lighten. Fold mixture back into whites. Sprinkle with hazelnut mixture and fold gently. Turn batter into prepared pan, spreading evenly. Bake until top is brown and tester inserted in center comes out clean, about 20 minutes. Cool cake completely in pan; cake will deflate.

For mousse: Melt chocolate with coffee in double boiler over gently simmering water; stir until smooth. Let cool.

Beat yolks into chocolate mixture 1 at a time. Blend in brandy. Beat whites until soft peaks form. Gradually add sugar and beat until stiff but not dry. Gently fold whites into chocolate mixture. Spread mousse onto cake. Cover and refrigerate until mousse is firm, several hours or overnight.

Just before serving, remove springform from cake. Sprinkle top with chocolate.

Chocolate Cream Cake

12 servings

1 12-ounce package semisweet chocolate chips
½ cup (1 stick) unsalted butter
6 eggs, separated, room temperature
1 cup sugar
½ cup finely chopped pecans
1 tablespoon Irish cream liqueur

½ teaspoon vanilla

Pinch of cream of tartar

2 cups whipping cream
¼ cup powdered sugar
2 tablespoons Irish cream liqueur
2 ounces chocolate curls (optional)

Preheat oven to 350°F. Grease and flour 10-inch springform pan. Melt chocolate chips and butter in top of double boiler over hot but not boiling water. Beat yolks in large bowl of electric mixer until very thick, about 5 minutes. Beat in ½ cup sugar 1 tablespoon at a time. Stir in melted chocolate, pecans, liqueur and vanilla.

Beat whites with cream of tartar in another large bowl until soft peaks form. Gradually add remaining ½ cup sugar and beat until stiff but not dry. Gently fold ¼ of whites into chocolate mixture, then fold chocolate mixture back into remaining whites. Pour into prepared pan. Bake 30 minutes. Reduce oven temperature to 275°F and continue baking 30 minutes. Turn off oven; let cake stand in oven for 30 minutes with door ajar.

Remove cake from oven. Dampen paper towel and place on top of cake for 5 minutes; remove towel (top of cake will crack and fall). Cool cake in pan.

Remove springform. Transfer cake to platter. Beat whipping cream in large bowl of electric mixer until soft peaks form. Beat in powdered sugar and liqueur. Spoon whipped cream onto top of cake and smooth evenly. Sprinkle with chocolate curls if desired. Refrigerate at least 6 hours. Let cake stand at room temperature 30 minutes before serving.

Chocolate Truffle Cake

8 to 10 servings

1 **pound semisweet chocolate (preferably imported), coarsely chopped**
10 **tablespoons (1¼ sticks) unsalted butter**

5 **eggs, separated, room temperature**

3 **cups whipping cream**
2 **tablespoons sugar**
½ **teaspoon vanilla**
   Grated chocolate

Melt chocolate and butter in double boiler over gently simmering water; stir until smooth. Pour into large bowl; cool slightly.

Preheat oven to 375°F. Generously butter 9-inch springform pan. Beat yolks to blend. Stir into chocolate mixture. Beat whites to stiff peaks. Gently fold ¼ of whites into chocolate mixture to loosen. Fold in remaining whites. Pour batter into prepared pan. Bake 12 minutes; do not overbake (cake will be loose). Cool completely in pan.

Just before serving, beat cream, sugar and vanilla to stiff peaks. Spoon over cake in pan, smoothing top. Remove springform. Garnish cake with grated chocolate.

Dagobert

An elegant finale showcasing layers of almond-coated pastry and a rich, bittersweet chocolate filling.

8 to 10 servings

Pastry Bases
 6 **tablespoons sugar**
⅓ **cup very finely ground almonds**
 4 **egg whites, room temperature**
⅛ **teaspoon cream of tartar**
1½ **cups sliced almonds**

Ganache
14 **ounces bittersweet (not unsweetened) or semisweet chocolate, finely chopped**
 1 **cup plus 2 tablespoons whipping cream**

¼ **cup coffee extract***

 5 **ounces bittersweet (not unsweetened) or semisweet chocolate, grated**
 1 **ounce bittersweet (not unsweetened) or semisweet chocolate, melted**
   Chocolate Marzipan Rose and Leaves**

For bases: Preheat oven to 375°F. Place dabs of butter in corners of three 12x9-inch baking pans. Line with parchment (butter will help hold in place). Mix 3 tablespoons sugar, ground almonds and 1 egg white in small bowl. Beat remaining 3 whites with cream of tartar in medium bowl until soft peaks form. Add 3 tablespoons sugar 1 tablespoon at a time and beat until stiff but not dry. Gently fold in almond mixture. Divide batter among prepared pans, spreading evenly to edges. Sprinkle with sliced almonds. Bake until light brown and springy to touch, about 15 minutes. Cool layers on parchment on racks. Refrigerate pastry bases while preparing ganache.

For ganache: Place 14 ounces chopped chocolate in large bowl. Bring cream to boil in medium saucepan. Pour over chocolate and stir until chocolate melts and is smooth. Cool to room temperature, stirring occasionally. Refrigerate until thick but not set, stirring occasionally. Using electric mixer, beat mixture until lighter in color and very soft peaks form, 3 to 5 minutes. Mix in coffee extract. Set aside.

To assemble: Peel parchment from base layers. Cut into three 8½x6-inch rectangles. Place one layer on 8½x6-inch cardboard rectangle, almond side up. Spread 1⅓ cups ganache evenly over layer. Top with another layer, almond side up, and spread with 1⅓ cups ganache. Top with third layer, almond side down. Spread remaining ganache over top and sides of dessert. Lightly set 7½x5-inch sheet of waxed paper in center of dessert, leaving 1-inch border. Cover border and side with grated chocolate. Carefully remove waxed paper. Spoon melted chocolate into parchment cone with small opening. Write "Dagobert" in center of cake. *(Can be prepared 1 day ahead and refrigerated.)* Place rose and leaves in one corner. Serve at room temperature.

*Available at specialty foods stores.

Chocolate Marzipan Rose and Leaves

Makes 1 rose and leaves

¼ cup marzipan

1 teaspoon unsweetened cocoa powder

Knead marzipan with cocoa until evenly colored. Roll into 1½x1-inch oval log. Cut into nine ⅛-inch-thick slices. Pinch edges of 1 slice to flatten to 2¼x1½-inch oval. Repeat with 5 more discs. Roll 1 oval up lengthwise into cylinder. Wrap second oval around cylinder. Pinch at base to seal. Repeat with remaining ovals, overlapping slightly. Open top of rose by curling petals back slightly. Cut base to flatten. Pinch remaining slices into leaf shapes. Score with lines to represent veins. *(Can be prepared 2 days ahead. Store in airtight container.)*

Nut-based Cakes

Lemon Almond Cake

---

8 servings

½ cup chopped slivered blanched almonds

1⅔ cups sifted almond meal
1⅔ cups sifted powdered sugar
  1 egg white, room temperature
  3 extra-large eggs, room temperature
  2 teaspoons Grand Marnier

2 teaspoons finely grated lemon peel
6 tablespoons cornstarch sifted with ½ teaspoon baking powder
6½ tablespoons unsalted butter, melted and cooled to lukewarm
  Powdered sugar

Preheat oven to 350°F. Butter 9x1½-inch or 8x2-inch round cake pan. Line bottom of pan with parchment paper; butter and flour paper. Press almonds around sides of baking pan; remove any that fall to bottom.

Mix almond meal and sugar in processor to very fine powder. With machine running, add egg white through feed tube and process to paste; mixture should stick together when pinched between fingers. Transfer to bowl of electric mixer. Beat in eggs 1 at a time. Continue beating until mixture is very light, about 10 minutes. Add Grand Marnier and lemon peel and beat 1 minute. Resift cornstarch mixture over and fold in gently, shaking spatula lightly after each fold to prevent lumping. Fold in butter. Pour batter into pan. Bake until tester inserted in center comes out clean, 40 to 45 minutes. Cool completely in pan. Invert cake onto platter. Sprinkle with powdered sugar before serving.

White Almond Layer Cake

A nut grinder gives almonds the light texture needed for this cake. If unavailable, grind almonds with ½ cup of the sugar in batches in blender or processor, stopping frequently to scrape down sides of container.

8 servings

Cake
- 1 cup cake flour
- ¼ cup cornstarch
- 2¼ teaspoons baking powder
- 1 cup blanched almonds (5 ounces), toasted and finely ground
- ½ cup (1 stick) butter, room temperature
- 1 cup plus 2 tablespoons sugar
- 1½ teaspoons vanilla
- ½ teaspoon almond extract
- ½ cup half and half
- 5 egg whites, room temperature
- ½ cup amaretto liqueur

Frosting
- ¾ cup apricot preserves
- 1 tablespoon amaretto liqueur
- 2⅔ cups whipping cream
- ¼ cup plus 2 tablespoons sugar
- 2 teaspoons vanilla
- ½ cup lightly toasted slivered almonds

For cake: Position rack in center of oven and preheat to 350°F. Butter and flour 9-inch springform pan. Sift together 1 cup flour, cornstarch and baking powder. Mix in ground almonds. Cream butter with sugar in large bowl of electric mixer until light and smooth. Blend in vanilla and almond extract. Beat in half and half alternately with almond mixture. Add whites and beat until mixture is pale, fluffy and looks slightly curdled. Turn into prepared pan, spreading evenly. Bake until tester inserted in center comes out clean and cake pulls away from sides of pan, 55 to 60 minutes. Let cake cool 5 minutes in pan. Remove springform and cool.

Pierce top of cake all over with toothpick. Sprinkle with ¼ cup amaretto. Return cake to pan. Cover with plastic wrap. Let stand 1 hour. Invert cake onto rack and unwrap. Pierce surface of cake all over with toothpick. Sprinkle with remaining amaretto. Return cake to pan. Cover with plastic wrap. Let stand 1 hour. *(Can be prepared 1 day ahead. Overwrap in foil and store at room temperature.)* Using serrated knife, slice cake horizontally into 3 layers.

For frosting: Heat preserves and amaretto in heavy small saucepan over low heat until preserves melt, stirring occasionally. Beat cream and sugar until soft peaks form. Blend in vanilla. Invert top cake layer onto platter. Spread with half of preserves. Cover with ¾-inch-thick layer of whipped cream. Top with second cake layer. Spread with remaining preserves. Cover with ¾-inch-thick layer of whipped cream. Top with third cake layer, pressing gently. Frost top and sides of cake with some of remaining whipped cream. Spoon remaining whipped cream into pastry bag fitted with large star tip. Pipe rosettes in vertical rows at 1-inch intervals on top of cake. Sprinkle almonds between rows. Refrigerate cake until ready to use.

Tips for Perfect Nut Cakes

Cakes that use ground nuts instead of flour as a main ingredient have an appealing crunchiness and an irresistible flavor that make them worth the extra effort. To achieve perfection every time, follow these simple tips.

- For best flavor, be sure to use fresh nuts. In many recipes, the nuts can be substituted with an equal weight of another variety of nut for a slightly different flavor.

- Nuts must be very finely ground. When using a processor, be careful not to grind them so long that they begin to cake. It is best to grind them in small batches, stopping occasionally to scrape down the sides of the work bowl. An electric nut grinder or hand rotary grater can also be used.

- For maximum lightness, beat egg whites last. Fold them into the other ingredients as soon as they are beaten, and immediately transfer the batter to a prepared pan and bake as directed.

- To fold in beaten egg whites quickly and efficiently, work clockwise while turning the mixing bowl counterclockwise: With your right hand, pull a flexible rubber spatula down through center of mixture to bottom of bowl. Move spatula under mixture toward left side of bowl, scraping bottom and side of bowl. (Reverse the directions if you are left-handed.) Repeat this motion several times. Add each batch of nuts or beaten whites just before the previous one is completely incorporated.

Ginger-Almond Gâteau with Fresh Strawberries

Choose berries of the same size for a professional-looking finish.

8 to 10 servings

Cake

- 1 cup all purpose flour
- 1 tablespoon ground ginger
- ¾ cup almonds, toasted and coarsely ground
- 2 tablespoons very finely chopped crystallized ginger
- 6 large eggs
- ½ teaspoon almond extract
- 1 cup sugar
- 6 tablespoons (¾ stick) unsalted butter, melted

Ginger Cream

- 2½ cups well-chilled whipping cream
- ½ teaspoon almond extract
- ¼ cup powdered sugar
- 2 tablespoons finely chopped crystallized ginger

- ½ cup sliced almonds, toasted
- 2 pints strawberries, halved lengthwise
- 3 tablespoons red currant jelly, melted

For cake: Position rack in center of oven and preheat to 350°F. Butter two 8-inch square baking pans. Line bottoms of pans with parchment or waxed paper. Butter paper; dust pans with flour. Combine 1 cup flour and ground ginger in medium bowl. Combine almonds and crystallized ginger in another bowl. Whisk eggs in bowl of electric mixer set over pan of simmering water until eggs are just warm to touch. Place bowl in mixer and beat eggs until light. Mix in almond extract. Gradually add sugar, beating until pale yellow and slowly dissolving ribbon forms when beaters are lifted.

Sift ⅓ of flour mixture over and sprinkle with ⅓ of almond mixture. Fold into eggs, using rubber spatula. Repeat with remaining flour mixture and almond mixture in 2 additions. Fold in butter ⅓ at a time. Divide batter between prepared pans. Bake until cakes are golden brown and springy to touch, about 20 minutes. Run knife between pan edges and cakes. Invert cakes onto rack and cool completely.

For cream: Whip cream until soft peaks form. Add almond extract. Gradually add powdered sugar and beat until stiff peaks form. Set aside 1¾ cups cream for sides of cake. Fold crystallized ginger into remaining cream.

Using serrated knife, cut cakes in half horizontally. Place 1 layer cut side up on platter. Spread 1 cup ginger cream over. Repeat with remaining layers and ginger cream, ending with cake cut side down. Spread reserved whipped cream over sides of cake. Press almonds into cream. Arrange berries cut side down in diagonal rows atop cake. Brush berries with currant jelly. *(Can be prepared 4 hours ahead and refrigerated.)* Serve ginger-almond gâteau at room temperature.

Spanish Cream Torte

8 servings

Torte
- 1 cup unblanched almonds (5 ounces), toasted
- 2 slices white bread
- 2 tablespoons all purpose flour
- 1 teaspoon cinnamon
- 7 eggs, separated, room temperature
- 1 cup sugar
- 1 teaspoon vanilla
- ½ teaspoon almond extract
- ¼ teaspoon cream of tartar

  Powdered sugar

Spanish Cream
- ½ cup (1 stick) unsalted butter
- ⅔ cup sugar
- 1 egg
- 1 egg yolk
- 2 tablespoons brandy
- 1 teaspoon vanilla
- ¼ teaspoon orange extract
- 1 cup plus 2 tablespoons whipping cream

Garnish
- ⅔ cup orange marmalade
- 1 tablespoon brandy
- ⅓ cup cream Sherry

- 1 navel orange, peeled and sliced
- ¼ cup unblanched almonds, toasted and chopped

For torte: Position rack in center of oven and preheat to 350°F. Line 17½x11½x1-inch rimmed baking sheet with foil. Grease and flour foil and rims of sheet, shaking off excess. Grind almonds with bread in processor. Turn into bowl. Stir in flour and cinnamon. Beat yolks and ¼ cup sugar in large bowl of electric mixer until light and fluffy. Blend in vanilla and almond extract. Using clean dry beaters, beat whites with cream of tartar until soft peaks form. Add remaining sugar 1 tablespoon at a time and beat until stiff but not dry. Fold ¼ of whites into yolk mixture to lighten. Fold remaining whites into yolk mixture alternately with almond mixture; do not overfold. Pour almond batter onto prepared baking sheet, spreading evenly. Bake until edges are dry, about 15 minutes.

Line work surface with waxed paper. Cover paper with powdered sugar. Invert torte onto prepared paper. Peel off foil. Let torte cool. Trim off ⅓ inch from all sides. Cut torte in half crosswise. Cut each piece in half crosswise.

For cream: Combine butter, sugar, egg and yolk in heavy medium saucepan over medium-high heat and whisk until butter melts, sugar dissolves and mixture is light and fluffy, about 5 minutes. Transfer to bowl. Set in larger bowl filled with water and ice and let cool until thick and stiff, stirring occasionally. Blend in brandy, vanilla and orange extract. Beat cream to stiff peaks. Gently beat in egg mixture. Cover and refrigerate at least 1 hour.

For garnish: Heat marmalade and brandy in heavy small saucepan over low heat until marmalade melts, stirring occasionally. Set 1 torte layer on platter. Sprinkle with Sherry. Brush with marmalade. Spread with ⅓-inch-thick layer of cream. Repeat layering with remaining ingredients, ending with cream. Chill at least 4 hours.

Before serving, arrange orange slices atop cake; sprinkle with almonds.

Gâteau Saint James

This cake becomes even more flavorful if refrigerated for one or two days.

8 to 10 servings

1 cup (2 sticks) unsalted butter, room temperature
1 cup plus 3 tablespoons sugar
5 eggs, separated
1 teaspoon almond extract
7 ounces unsweetened chocolate, ground

7 ounces blanched almonds, ground
½ teaspoon cream of tartar

Powdered sugar (garnish)

Preheat oven to 325°F. Butter 9x2-inch cake pan. Line bottom with a circle of parchment paper and oil lightly.

Cream butter, sugar, egg yolks and almond extract until light and fluffy. Add chocolate and almonds and stir until well combined. Beat egg whites until foamy. Add cream of tartar and beat until stiff but not dry. Add large spoonful to butter mixture and stir to loosen batter. Gently fold in remaining whites. Turn into prepared pan and bake until edges of cake shrink slightly from pan (cake will be soft in center), 40 to 45 minutes. Let cool completely in pan. Invert onto serving platter and remove parchment; if cake seems oily, blot with paper towels to remove.

Just before ready to serve, cut out Saint James pattern (rising sun; see photograph) from waxed paper. Set over cake and sprinkle with powdered sugar. Gently remove paper and serve.

California Harvest Torte

A sumptuous chocolate cake with a bright fruit counterpoint. For best flavor, bake it one day ahead.

10 servings

Cake
3 tablespoons minced dried apricots
¼ cup brandy
⅛ teaspoon almond extract
6 ounces semisweet or bittersweet (not unsweetened) chocolate, finely chopped
½ cup (1 stick) unsalted butter, cut into small pieces
3 eggs, separated, room temperature
½ cup plus 3 tablespoons sugar

⅔ cup ground blanched almonds (about 3 ounces)
¼ cup all purpose flour
¼ teaspoon (scant) cream of tartar

Caramelized Apricots
12 bamboo skewers
12 small dried apricots of similar size
½ cup sugar
¼ cup water

Chocolate Glaze*

For cake: Preheat oven to 375°F. Grease 8-inch-diameter cake pan with 2-inch sides. Line bottom with parchment or waxed paper. Soak apricots in brandy and almond extract. Melt chocolate with butter in top of double boiler over barely simmering water; stir until smooth. Remove from heat. Beat yolks and ½ cup sugar until pale yellow and slowly dissolving ribbon forms when beaters are lifted. Beat in chocolate, almonds and flour. Fold in apricots with soaking liquid. Using clean dry beaters, beat whites with cream of tartar until soft peaks form. Add remaining 3 tablespoons sugar 1 tablespoon at a time and beat until stiff but not dry. Gently fold ⅓ of whites into batter to lighten; fold in remaining whites. Turn batter into prepared pan. Bake until tester inserted in center comes out with moist crumbs, about 35 minutes. Cool cake in pan. Wrap tightly and let stand 1 day at room temperature. *(Can be prepared 3 days ahead. Do not refrigerate.)*

For apricots: Using skewer like lollipop stick, push into thick edge of each apricot just far enough to secure. Prop skewers against edge of bowl, apricot ends up. Cook sugar and water in heavy small saucepan over low heat, swirling pan occasionally, until sugar dissolves. Increase heat to medium and cook until syrup is mahogany. Remove from heat. Immediately dip apricots in syrup and return to rim of bowl. Let stand until syrup is almost firm. Gently remove skewers. Snip off any caramel "tails" with scissors.

Run knife between cake and pan edges. Press on raised cake edges to level. Invert onto 8-inch cardboard round. Spread edges with just enough Chocolate Glaze to smooth any imperfections; be careful to keep crumbs out of remaining glaze. Reheat remaining glaze over barely simmering water until smooth and just pourable but not thin and watery. Strain through fine sieve. Place cake on bakery turntable or plate. Pour glaze into center of cake. Using dry metal spatula, spread over top and sides of cake, working as little as possible. Transfer cake to rack. Arrange caramelized apricots around upper edge. Let glaze set. Serve cake same day at room temperature.

*Chocolate Glaze

Makes about 1¼ cups

½ cup (1 stick) unsalted butter, cut into small pieces
6 ounces semisweet or bittersweet (not unsweetened) chocolate, finely chopped

1 tablespoon corn syrup

Melt butter and chocolate with corn syrup in double boiler over barely simmering water, stirring until smooth. Cool until almost set but still spreadable.

Chocolate Almond Cake with Grand Marnier

8 to 10 servings

Almond Cake
4 ounces semisweet chocolate, chopped
¼ cup (½ stick) unsalted butter

½ cup blanched almonds (about 2¼ ounces)
⅔ cup sugar
3 tablespoons cornstarch
3 eggs, separated, room temperature

2 tablespoons Grand Marnier
¼ teaspoon cream of tartar

Grand Marnier Whipped Cream
¾ cup whipping cream, well chilled
1½ teaspoons sugar
1½ teaspoons Grand Marnier
½ ounce semisweet chocolate

For cake: Position rack in center of oven and preheat to 350°F. Butter 9x1½-inch round cake pan. Line base with parchment or foil. Lightly butter paper. Melt chocolate and butter in large heatproof bowl set in pan of hot water over low heat. Stir until smooth. Cool until tepid, about 10 minutes.

Grind nuts with 3 tablespoons sugar in processor as finely as possible. Transfer to small bowl. Thoroughly mix in 4 tablespoons sugar and cornstarch. Stir into chocolate. Beat in yolks with wooden spoon until mixture is smooth and thick. Stir in Grand Marnier. Beat whites with cream of tartar in large bowl until soft peaks form. Beat in remaining scant ¼ cup sugar 1 tablespoon at a time. Continue beating until whites are stiff but not dry. Fold ⅓ of whites into chocolate mixture to lighten. Spoon chocolate mixture back into whites and fold just until blended and no white streaks remain.

Pour batter into prepared pan. Bake until tester inserted in center comes out clean, about 25 minutes. Run thin-bladed flexible knife around sides of cake; turn out onto rack and remove paper. Invert again onto another rack. Cool completely. Refrigerate at least 1 hour before frosting. *(Can be prepared 3 days ahead to this point.)*

For whipped cream: Beat cream with sugar and Grand Marnier in chilled bowl until firm peaks form. Invert cake smooth side up onto platter. Spread cream on sides and top of cake. Grate chocolate over top. *(Can be prepared 8 hours ahead and refrigerated.)* Serve cake at room temperature.

Brazil Nut and Orange Cake

10 servings

2 cups plus 2 tablespoons (about 10 ounces) Brazil nuts

¾ cup plus 2 tablespoons sugar
¼ cup all purpose flour

5 eggs, separated, room temperature

1 tablespoon strained fresh orange juice
1 teaspoon grated orange peel
¼ teaspoon cream of tartar

Powdered sugar

Position rack in center of oven and preheat to 350°F. Toast nuts in shallow baking pan 10 minutes. Transfer ⅓ of nuts to large strainer. Turn off heat and leave remaining nuts in oven. Rub nuts against strainer with terrycloth towel to remove most of skins. Transfer nuts to medium bowl. Repeat with remaining nuts in 2 batches. Allow to cool completely.

Preheat oven to 325°F. Butter 9-inch springform pan. Line base with parchment or foil. Butter paper. Dust pan with flour. Grind ½ of nuts with 3 tablespoons sugar in processor as finely as possible. Transfer to another medium bowl. Repeat with remaining nuts and 3 more tablespoons sugar. Sift flour onto nuts and blend well.

Beat yolks with ¼ cup sugar in large bowl until pale yellow and slowly dissolving ribbon forms when beaters are lifted, about 5 minutes. Beat in juice and peel. Beat whites with cream of tartar in another large bowl to soft peaks. Beat in remaining ¼ cup sugar 1 tablespoon at a time. Continue beating until whites are stiff but not dry. Fold ⅓ of nut mixture into yolks. Gently fold in ⅓ of whites. Repeat with remaining nuts and whites in 2 batches, folding just until blended and no white streaks remain.

Spread batter evenly in prepared pan. Bake until tester inserted in center comes out clean, about 45 minutes. Cool in pan on rack 10 minutes. Run thin-bladed flexible knife around sides of cake; invert onto rack and remove paper. Invert again onto another rack. Cool completely. *(Can be prepared 2 days ahead. Wrap tightly and refrigerate.)* Invert cake onto platter. Dust decoratively with powdered sugar. Serve cake at room temperature.

Austrian Hazelnut Cake

12 to 14 servings

Cake
- 8 eggs, separated
- ½ teaspoon cream of tartar
- 1½ cups sugar

- 1 teaspoon vanilla
- 1½ cups finely ground hazelnuts
- ⅓ cup very fine breadcrumbs

  Buttercream *or* Whipped Cream
  Filling

Buttercream
- 1¼ cups sugar
- ½ cup water
- 6 egg yolks

- 1 pound (4 sticks) unsalted butter, cut into pieces, room temperature
- 3 tablespoons instant coffee powder
- 3 tablespoons dark rum
- 1 tablespoon unsweetened cocoa

Whipped Cream Filling
- 1 pint (2 cups) whipping cream, well chilled
- ⅓ cup powdered sugar
- 1½ teaspoons vanilla

- ¼ cup (about) dark rum
- ½ cup ground toasted hazelnuts (decoration)

Preheat oven to 350°F. Butter three 9-inch springform pans. Beat egg whites until foamy. Add cream of tartar and continue beating until soft peaks form. Gradually add ¾ cup sugar and beat until very stiff but not dry.

Beat egg yolks with remaining ¾ cup sugar until thick and pale yellow. Blend in vanilla. Combine hazelnuts and breadcrumbs. Add to yolk mixture and beat well. Stir in 1 cup egg whites to loosen batter. Gently fold in remaining whites; *do not overfold*.

Divide batter among prepared pans, smoothing tops with spatula. Bake until edges of cake shrink slightly from pan, about 30 to 35 minutes. Cool in pans.

For buttercream: Combine sugar and water in heavy small saucepan. Bring to boil, stirring just until sugar is dissolved, and let boil 5 minutes. Meanwhile, beat egg yolks until thick and lemon colored. Beating constantly, gradually add boiling syrup and continue beating until mixture is cool. Gradually beat in butter and remaining ingredients. Chill briefly.

For cream filling: Combine cream, sugar and vanilla and beat until very thick.

To assemble: Remove cake from pans. Brush each layer with rum. Set one layer on serving plate and cover with some of buttercream or whipped cream. Repeat with remaining layers. Frost top and sides of assembled cake and sprinkle with hazelnuts. Chill until ready to serve.

Chocolate Hazelnut Cake

8 to 10 servings

Chocolate Hazelnut Cake
- 4 ounces semisweet chocolate, chopped
- 1½ teaspoons instant espresso powder, dissolved in 1 tablespoon boiling water and cooled
- ⅔ cup sugar
- ½ cup (1 stick) unsalted butter, room temperature
- 6 eggs, separated, room temperature
- ½ cup toasted husked ground hazelnuts
- ¼ cup Frangelico liqueur
  Pinch of salt
  Pinch of cream of tartar

- ¾ cup plus 2 tablespoons all purpose flour
- 2 tablespoons cornstarch

Chocolate Frosting
- 1½ ounces semisweet chocolate, chopped
- ½ teaspoon mocha extract
- ¼ cup (½ stick) unsalted butter, cut into ½-inch pieces

  Hazelnuts, mint leaves and candied violets (garnish)
  Frangelico Cream*

For cake: Position rack in lower third of oven and preheat to 350°F. Butter and flour 9-inch round cake pan, shaking out excess. Melt chocolate with espresso in top of double boiler set over simmering water. Combine sugar and butter in large bowl of electric mixer and beat until pale yellow and sugar is dissolved; about 5 minutes. Beat in yolks one at a time. Mix in hazelnuts, liqueur and chocolate mixture. Beat egg whites with salt and cream of tartar in large bowl until stiff but not dry. Fold ¼ of whites into yolk mixture to lighten. Spoon remaining whites on top. Sift flour and cornstarch over whites and gently but thoroughly fold mixture together. Pour into prepared pan. Bake until tester inserted near sides comes out clean, about 25 minutes (center may still be moist). Cool in pan on rack.

For frosting: Melt chocolate in small bowl set in hot water. Add extract; blend in butter until smooth. Set bowl in ice and stir mixture until thick.

Invert cake onto platter. Spread frosting over top and sides. Garnish top with nuts and leaves. Place violets in center. Serve with Frangelico Cream.

*Frangelico Cream

Makes about 1½ cups

4 egg yolks, room temperature	1 cup nonfat milk
¼ cup sugar	¼ cup Frangelico liqueur
Pinch of salt	

Combine yolks, sugar and salt in large saucepan and whisk until light colored and creamy, about 3 minutes. Add milk in steady stream, place over medium heat and cook, stirring constantly, until mixture is thickened and coats back of wooden spoon. Blend in liqueur. Strain. Serve warm.

Spirited Macadamia Nut Cake

A special touch is the addition of nut liqueur to the filling and topping.

12 servings

Macadamia Nut Cake
2⅓ cups unsalted macadamia nuts (about 10 ounces)
¾ cup plus 2 tablespoons sugar
¼ cup all purpose flour

5 eggs, separated, room temperature
¾ teaspoon vanilla
¼ teaspoon cream of tartar

Macadamia Nut Filling
6 tablespoons (¾ stick) unsalted butter, room temperature
5 tablespoons powdered sugar, sifted
1 egg yolk

1 tablespoon macadamia nut liqueur
½ cup unsalted macadamia nuts (about 2 ounces)

Whipped Cream Topping
1 cup whipping cream, well chilled
1 tablespoon sugar
2 tablespoons macadamia nut liqueur
Chopped toasted unsalted macadamia nuts

For cake: Position rack in center of oven and preheat to 325°F. Butter 9-inch spring-form pan. Line base with parchment or foil. Butter paper. Dust pan with flour. Grind half of nuts with 3 tablespoons sugar in processor as finely as possible. Transfer to medium bowl. Repeat with remaining nuts and 3 more tablespoons sugar. Sift flour onto nuts and blend well.

Beat yolks with ¼ cup sugar in large bowl until pale yellow and slowly dissolving ribbon forms when beaters are lifted, about 5 minutes. Beat in vanilla. Beat whites with cream of tartar in another large bowl until soft peaks form. Beat in remaining ¼ cup sugar 1 tablespoon at a time. Continue beating until whites are stiff but not dry. Fold ⅓ of nut mixture into yolks. Gently fold in ⅓ of whites. Repeat with remaining nuts and whites in 2 batches, folding just until blended and no white streaks remain.

Spread batter evenly in prepared pan. Bake until tester inserted in center comes out clean, about 52 minutes. Cool in pan on rack 10 minutes. Run thin-bladed flexible knife around sides of cake; invert onto rack and remove paper. Invert again onto another rack. Cool completely. *(Can be prepared 2 days ahead to this point. Wrap tightly with plastic and refrigerate.)*

For filling: Beat butter and ¼ cup powdered sugar in small bowl until smooth. Beat in yolk and then liqueur. Grind nuts with remaining 1 tablespoon powdered sugar in processor until fine. Stir into butter mixture. Cut cake in half horizontally, using long serrated knife. Spread filling over bottom layer. Place second layer smooth side up on top. Refrigerate 1 hour.

For topping: Beat cream with sugar in chilled bowl until soft peaks form. Add liqueur and beat until firm peaks form. Spread cream on sides and top of cake. (Reserve some cream for garnish if desired. Spoon into pastry bag fitted with star tip. Pipe cream decoratively atop cake.) Sprinkle center of cake with chopped nuts. *(Can be frosted 4 hours ahead and refrigerated.)* Serve cake at room temperature.

French Apple Pudding Cake with Lemon Glaze

For transporting, put this cake back into its springform ring.

8 servings

6 **eggs**
1 **cup sugar**
1½ **cups finely chopped pecans**
1 **cup graham cracker crumbs**
1 **teaspoon baking powder**
½ **teaspoon salt**
1 **large apple, peeled, cored and grated**
1 **tablespoon grated lemon peel**

1 **tablespoon fresh lemon juice**

1 **cup sifted powdered sugar**
4 **teaspoons (or more) fresh lemon juice**
¼ **cup coarsely chopped pecans**

Preheat oven to 350°F. Butter 10-inch springform pan. In large bowl of electric mixer, beat eggs with 1 cup sugar until pale yellow and slowly dissolving ribbon forms when beaters are lifted. Combine 1½ cups pecans, crumbs, baking powder and salt and fold into egg mixture; do not overmix. Fold in apple, lemon peel and 1 tablespoon lemon juice. Pour into prepared pan, smoothing top with rubber spatula. Bake until tester inserted in center comes out clean and cake is springy to touch, about 40 minutes. Cool cake in pan on rack. Remove springform.

Combine powdered sugar and 4 teaspoons lemon juice in small bowl and stir to combine. Add more lemon juice if necessary for proper drizzling consistency. Spoon glaze over cake. Sprinkle with ¼ cup pecans.

Maple Pecan Torte with Chocolate Filling

8 to 10 servings

6 **eggs, separated**
2 **teaspoons distilled white vinegar**
3½ **cups pecans (14 ounces), lightly toasted**
1 **1-inch-thick slice soft white bread, quartered**
¾ **cup sugar**
½ **cup firmly packed light brown sugar**

1½ **teaspoons baking powder**
¼ **teaspoon salt**
2 **tablespoons bourbon**
1 **teaspoon maple flavoring**

Chocolate Filling*
Maple Buttercream**
Lightly toasted pecan halves

Position rack in center of oven and preheat to 350°F. Butter two 9-inch round cake pans. Line bottoms with waxed paper; butter paper.

Beat egg whites in processor until foamy, about 8 seconds. With machine running, pour vinegar through feed tube and process until whites are stiff and hold their shape, about 2 minutes. Transfer whites to small bowl, using rubber spatula. Wipe out work bowl with paper towel. Add ½ cup pecans to processor and chop using 4 on/off turns, then process continuously until minced, about 8 seconds. Remove from work bowl and set aside. (Do not clean work bowl.) Combine remaining 3 cups pecans, bread, both sugars, baking powder and salt in work bowl and process until pecans are ground, about 1 minute, stopping once to scrape down sides of work bowl. Add yolks, bourbon and maple flavoring and blend 30 seconds. Add ¼ of whites and process until thoroughly blended, about 30 seconds. Add remaining whites and blend using 3 on/off turns. Run spatula around inside of work bowl. Blend just until whites are incorporated, using 2 to 3 on/off turns (some streaks of white may remain; do not overprocess batter).

Divide batter between prepared pans. Bake until tester inserted in centers comes out clean, about 25 minutes. Let cool in pans 10 minutes. Invert onto racks; remove waxed paper. Cool completely before frosting.

To assemble: Place one cake layer smooth side up on platter. Slide waxed paper strips under cake to keep plate clean. Spread Chocolate Filling over top of cake. Arrange second layer smooth side up on top. Spread very thin film of buttercream over top and sides of cake. Refrigerate until buttercream is set, about 20 minutes. Spread remaining buttercream over top and sides of cake, using long thin spatula. Press reserved chopped pecans into sides of cake. Garnish top of cake with pecan halves. *(Can be prepared 2 days ahead, covered and refrigerated. Bring torte to room temperature before serving.)*

*Chocolate Filling

Makes about 1 cup

¼ cup (½ stick) unsalted butter
2 tablespoons strong brewed coffee

2 ounces unsweetened chocolate, broken into pieces

1 cup powdered sugar
1 teaspoon maple flavoring

Melt butter with coffee in heavy small saucepan; keep at simmer.

Chop chocolate in processor about 6 on/off turns, then process continuously until finely ground. With machine running, pour hot butter mixture through feed tube and process until chocolate is melted and completely smooth, stopping once to scrape down sides of work bowl. Add sugar and maple flavoring and process until smooth, about 30 seconds. Let stand at room temperature until thick enough to spread, about 4 minutes.

**Maple Buttercream

Makes about 1¾ cups

2¼ cups powdered sugar
¾ cup (1½ sticks) unsalted butter, cut into 6 pieces, room temperature
2 tablespoons cold coffee

2 tablespoons sour cream
1 tablespoon vanilla
1 teaspoon maple flavoring
   Pinch of salt

Combine sugar and butter in processor until smooth, about 1 minute, stopping once to scrape down sides of work bowl. Add remaining ingredients and blend 30 seconds. *(Can be prepared 3 days ahead, covered and refrigerated. Let buttercream stand at room temperature until soft enough to spread.)*

Chocolate Apricot Pecan Torte

A great do-ahead dessert. The pretty apricot roses are surprisingly easy to make.

14 to 16 servings

Chocolate-Apricot Cake
- ⅓ cup Cognac
- 1¼ cups dried apricots (about 6 ounces), cut into ¼-inch pieces
- 1 tablespoon butter, room temperature
- 3 tablespoons dry breadcrumbs
- ¾ cup (1½ sticks) unsalted butter, room temperature
- 1 cup sugar
- 5 eggs, room temperature
- 6 ounces semisweet chocolate, melted and cooled
- 1½ teaspoons vanilla
- ⅔ cup dry breadcrumbs
- 1½ cups coarsely chopped pecans
- 1 tablespoon all purpose flour

Chocolate Icing
- ½ cup unsweetened cocoa powder
- ½ cup sugar
- ½ cup whipping cream
- ¼ cup (½ stick) unsalted butter, cut into small pieces

Apricot Glaze
- 2 tablespoons (about) Cognac
- ½ cup apricot jam
- ½ cup pecan halves (optional)
  Apricot Roses*
  Chocolate Leaves**

For cake: Heat Cognac in medium saucepan until just hot. Remove from heat and mix in apricots. Let soak 15 minutes. Strain apricots, reserving any soaking liquid for glaze.

Preheat oven to 375°F. Butter 8½-inch springform pan with 1 tablespoon butter. Dust with 3 tablespoons breadcrumbs. Using electric mixer, cream butter until light and fluffy. Gradually beat in sugar. Beat in eggs one at a time (mixture may look curdled). Add chocolate and vanilla. Mix in ⅔ cup breadcrumbs. Combine pecans and flour and blend into batter. Fold in apricots. Spoon batter into prepared pan. Bake until tester inserted in center comes out clean, about 50 minutes. Cool in pan on rack.

Run knife around edge of cake. Invert onto platter. Slide sheets of waxed paper under edges of cake.

For icing: Stir all ingredients in top of double boiler over simmering water until mixture is shiny and smooth, about 5 minutes. Cool icing for 5 minutes, stirring occasionally.

Pour icing over cake, tilting cake to cover evenly. Using thin flat spatula, spread icing over top and sides of cake. Refrigerate until icing is firm.

For glaze: Add enough Cognac to soaking liquid reserved from apricots to measure 2 tablespoons. Combine with jam in heavy small saucepan. Stir over medium-low heat until melted. Strain through fine sieve into bowl. Cool until tepid, 5 minutes.

Pour glaze over top of cake. Using thin metal spatula, spread evenly (do not let any drip down sides). Arrange pecans around upper edge of cake, ends touching. Discard paper. Refrigerate cake until glaze is set. *(Cake can be prepared up to 1 day ahead.)*

Arrange Apricot Roses in center of torte. Place large chocolate leaf between each flower. Place smaller leaf between each large leaf. Let stand at room temperature 1 hour before serving.

*Apricot Roses

Makes 3

12 moist dried apricots

Roll each apricot out, sticky side down, between 2 sheets of waxed paper to thickness of ¹⁄₁₆ inch. Roll one up tightly, sticky side in, to form tight center bud of rose. Wrap another apricot around bud, sticky side in, pressing gently to adhere. Repeat with 2 more apricots, overlapping half of each previous one. Gently bend top of outer 3 apricots outward to form petals. Place toothpick horizontally through base of rose. Cut off apricot below toothpick to form flat base. Repeat with remaining apricots. Place roses on plate and freeze 30 minutes. *(Can be prepared 3 days ahead. Cover tightly and refrigerate.)* Discard toothpicks before arranging roses on cake.

**Chocolate Leaves

Makes 6

3 ounces semisweet chocolate, melted
3 large rose leaves with stems

3 medium rose leaves with stems

Spread chocolate over veined side of each leaf, being careful not to drip on edges. Place on plate chocolate side up. Freeze until just firm, about 10 minutes. Starting at stem end, gently peel leaf away from chocolate, freezing briefly if too soft to work. *(Chocolate Leaves can be prepared 1 week ahead and refrigerated. Wrap tightly.)*

World's Finest Chocolate Gâteau

Adapted from a recipe by Simone Beck, this cake improves with age, so make it at least one day ahead.

8 servings

2 tablespoons raisins
2 tablespoons golden raisins
¼ cup Calvados

7 ounces bittersweet or semisweet chocolate
3 tablespoons water
½ cup (1 stick) unsalted butter, cut into 8 pieces, room temperature
3 eggs, separated, room temperature
⅔ cup sugar

⅔ cup ground pecans
4½ tablespoons cake flour
Pinch of salt
Pinch of cream of tartar

3 ounces bittersweet or semisweet chocolate
3 tablespoons powdered sugar
3 tablespoons butter, cut into 3 pieces, room temperature

Soak raisins in Calvados 1 hour.

Preheat oven to 375°F. Butter 9-inch round cake pan. Line bottom with parchment or waxed paper; butter paper. Melt 7 ounces chocolate with 3 tablespoons water in double boiler over simmering water, stirring until smooth. Remove from over water. Stir in ½ cup butter 1 piece at a time. Beat yolks with sugar in large bowl of electric mixer until pale yellow and slowly dissolving ribbon forms when beaters are lifted. Fold in chocolate. Combine pecans and flour. Stir into batter. Blend in raisins and Calvados. Beat whites with salt and cream of tartar until stiff but not dry. Fold ⅓ of whites into batter to lighten. Fold back into remaining whites. Pour batter into pan. Bake until top of cake is firm to the touch, about 25 minutes. Cool 10 minutes. Invert onto rack and cool completely. Remove paper.

Melt remaining 3 ounces chocolate in double boiler over barely simmering water. Stir in powdered sugar. Add remaining 3 tablespoons butter 1 piece at a time, blending until smooth. Spread on top and sides of cake. Let stand until glaze is set, about 30 minutes. Refrigerate until firm, then wrap in foil and refrigerate overnight. Let stand at room temperature 15 minutes before serving. *(Can be refrigerated up to 3 days or frozen up to 2 months.)*

Chocolate Irish Whiskey Cake

Pecans and raisins add an interesting texture to this rich liquor-laced cake.

8 to 10 servings

Cake
- ¾ cup (1½ sticks) unsalted butter
- 1 cup sugar
- 6 eggs, separated, room temperature
- 5 ounces imported bittersweet or semisweet chocolate, melted
- ½ cup Irish whiskey
- 2½ cups ground pecans
- 1 cup raisins
- ¼ cup all purpose flour, sifted

Glaze
- 2½ cups powdered sugar
- ¼ cup water
- ½ cup (1 stick) unsalted butter
- ½ cup whipping cream
- 2 cups (scant) unsweetened cocoa powder, sifted
- ½ cup (about) light corn syrup
- Pecan halves

For cake: Preheat oven to 325°F. Butter and flour 9-inch round cake pan. Using electric mixer, cream butter and ¾ cup sugar. Beat in yolks. Stir in chocolate and whiskey. Fold in pecans, raisins and flour. Using clean, dry beaters, beat whites until soft peaks form. Gradually add remaining sugar and beat until stiff but not dry. Gently fold ¼ of whites into chocolate mixture to lighten. Fold in remaining whites. Turn batter into prepared pan. Reduce oven temperature to 300°F. Bake cake until puffed and firm, about 1 hour; top may crack. Cool in pan 10 minutes. Remove from pan and cool completely on wire rack.

For glaze: In heavy medium saucepan, dissolve sugar in enough water to form smooth paste. Add butter and cream. Bring to boil over very low heat. Remove from heat. Add cocoa powder and whisk until smooth. Add enough corn syrup to thin to coating consistency. Pour glaze over cake, smoothing surfaces. Decorate with pecans. Serve cake at room temperature.

Chocolate-glazed Pistachio Cake

12 servings

- 3 cups shelled pistachio nuts (1 pound), toasted
- 2½ cups all purpose flour

- 1½ cups (3 sticks) butter, room temperature
- 2 cups sugar
- 6 egg yolks, beaten to blend, room temperature
- 1 cup milk
- ¼ cup Cointreau or Triple Sec
- 1 tablespoon (generous) grated lemon peel
- 1 tablespoon vanilla

- 6 egg whites, room temperature
- 1 teaspoon cream of tartar

- 1 pound semisweet chocolate, chopped
- 2 cups whipping cream

- 1¾ cups powdered sugar
- 1½ egg whites
- 1½ teaspoons fresh lemon juice

- 10 ounces white chocolate, chopped
- 48 ivy or other large waxy leaves with stems, washed and dried
- 24 white Jordan almonds

Grind ½ cup nuts in processor to fine powder (not paste). Set aside. Coarsely chop remaining 2½ cups nuts in processor using several on/off turns. Toss ground nuts with 2 tablespoons flour.

Cream butter and sugar in bowl of heavy-duty mixer. Mix in nut powder and remaining flour. Blend in yolks, milk, liqueur, lemon peel and vanilla.

Position rack in center of oven and preheat to 300°F. Lightly butter and flour 3-quart 7-inch-high tube pan. Beat 6 egg whites with cream of tartar until stiff but not dry. Gently fold whites into batter. Fold in chopped nuts. Pour batter into prepared pan; do not shake to settle batter. Bake until golden and tester inserted in center comes out clean, about 90 minutes; cake will crack on top. Cool in pan on rack 30 minutes. Turn out onto rack and cool completely. *(Can be prepared 1 day ahead to this point. Wrap in plastic and store at room temperature.)*

Melt semisweet chocolate in top of large double boiler above very gently simmering water. Bring cream to boil in saucepan and beat into chocolate until smooth. Cool mixture completely. Refrigerate glaze overnight.

Set cake on rack over tray. Warm glaze in top of double boiler above very gently simmering water. Stir with wooden spoon until pliable enough to whisk, then whisk until shiny. Pour glaze over cake, including center cavity. Spread with thin spatula to cover any unglazed areas. Refrigerate cake until chocolate glaze is firm.

Beat 1 cup powdered sugar, 1½ egg whites and lemon juice in bowl of electric mixer until soft peaks form. Add remaining sugar and continue beating until whites are stiff. Spoon icing into pastry bag fitted with No. 2 round tip. Set cake on platter. Pipe trellis pattern on top and sides of cake. Reserve icing.

Melt white chocolate in top of double boiler over gently simmering water. Spread ⅛-inch layer of chocolate on underside of leaves (do not let chocolate drip onto top of leaves). Freeze until chocolate is firm, about 10 minutes. Dip hands in ice water and dry. Remove leaf from chocolate by pulling gently from stem. Use remaining icing to attach leaves and almonds in clusters to base and top of cake.

Citrus Prune Cake

10 to 12 servings

2¼ cups pitted prunes (12 ounces)
2 cups prune juice

8 eggs, separated, room temperature
1½ cups sugar
1 tablespoon fresh lemon juice
2 teaspoons grated lemon peel
2 teaspoons vanilla (optional)

¾ cup matzo cake meal
¼ cup potato starch
1 cup walnuts (4½ ounces), finely chopped

½ teaspoon salt
Prune Sauce*

Combine prunes and prune juice in medium saucepan and bring to boil. Reduce heat and simmer until prunes are very tender, about 15 minutes. Drain well, reserving liquid for sauce. Puree prunes. Measure 1 cup puree for cake. Reserve remainder for sauce.

Preheat oven to 350°F. Using electric mixer, beat yolks and ¾ cup sugar until slowly dissolving ribbon forms when beaters are lifted, about 5 minutes. Gently fold in 1 cup prune puree, lemon juice, peel and vanilla. Sift together cake meal and potato starch. Fold into yolk mixture. Fold in nuts.

Using clean, dry beaters, beat whites with salt until soft peaks form. Gradually add remaining ¾ cup sugar and beat until stiff but not dry. Gently fold ⅓ of whites into yolk mixture to lighten. Fold mixture back into whites. Turn into ungreased 10-inch tube pan. Bake until tester inserted in center comes out clean, about 45 minutes. Invert onto rack and cool completely. To serve, cut cake into thin slices. Top each with 2 to 3 tablespoons sauce.

*Prune Sauce

Makes about 1¾ cups

Reserved prune puree and liquid
from cake
¼ cup honey

2 tablespoons (or more) dry red wine
½ teaspoon grated lemon peel

Warm puree, liquid, honey, 2 tablespoons wine and lemon peel in heavy small saucepan over low heat. If thinner consistency is desired, stir in 1 to 2 teaspoons more wine. Serve Prune Sauce warm.

Walnut-Wine Syrup Cake

Delicious served with a fresh fruit compote.

12 servings

Syrup
1 cup sugar
¾ cup water
¾ cup semidry white wine
   Peel of 1 medium orange
1 3-inch cinnamon stick
4 whole cloves

2 tablespoons fresh orange juice
1 teaspoon vanilla (optional)
2 cups walnuts (8 ounces), chopped
¾ cup matzo cake meal
½ teaspoon cinnamon
⅛ teaspoon salt

Cake
9 eggs, separated, room temperature
⅔ cup sugar

For syrup: Heat all ingredients in saucepan over low heat until sugar dissolves, swirling pan occasionally.

Increase heat to high and bring to boil. Reduce heat to medium and boil 10 minutes. Cool completely. Discard peel and spices. Set syrup aside.

For cake: Preheat oven to 350°F. Grease 9x13-inch baking pan. Using electric mixer, beat yolks and ⅓ cup sugar in large bowl until slowly dissolving ribbon forms when beaters are lifted, about 5 minutes. Blend in orange juice and vanilla. Stir in walnuts, cake meal and cinnamon. Using clean, dry beaters, beat whites with salt until soft peaks form. Gradually add remaining ⅓ cup sugar and beat until stiff but not dry. Gently fold ⅓ of whites into yolk mixture to lighten. Fold mixture back into whites. Turn into prepared pan. Bake until top is deep golden brown and tester inserted in center comes out barely moist, about 40 minutes. Set pan on rack. Immediately pour syrup over cake. Cool completely before serving.

Chocolate Raspberry Cloud Roll

Irwin Horowitz

Clockwise from top: Chocolate Mousse Hazelnut Cake; Lemon-Lime Roll; Banana Nutmeg Cake with Caramelized Brown Sugar Sauce

Brian Leatart

Chocolate Chip-Coffee Ice Cream Cake

Irwin Horowitz

Chocolate Cake with Blueberries

Irwin Horowitz

Chocolate Butterscotch Torte

Aaron Rezny

5 ❧ Special Occasion Cakes

In the early days of formal cookery, any chef worthy of the title had to be able to come up with an unusual and gorgeous dessert—what we like to call a showstopper. This often involved creating intricate Biblical scenes or gigantic figures of pastry and spun sugar. An average banquet dessert could have required dozens of pounds of nuts, candied fruits and other sweets. Luckily, today, a well-made cake, of quality ingredients and creatively decorated with, for example, simple chocolate curls and fruit, will win acclaim for any hostess. So, for contemporary showstoppers, we offer the recipes in this chapter.

The nice thing about these beautiful desserts is that much of the work can be accomplished in advance. For most, the cake, filling and decorations can all be prepared well ahead of time, refrigerated or frozen, and then assembled, sometimes as much as a day ahead. Some of our most spectacular do-ahead cakes include the lovely Princess Cake (page 98), layered with raspberry jam, vanilla custard and wrapped in pale green marzipan; Chocolate Cranberry Trifle Cake (page 106), chocolate sponge with cranberry filling and chocolate mousse, served with a Grand Marnier sauce; and White Christmas Mousse Torte (page 110), an elegant, sliced jelly-roll creation of butter sponge cake, white chocolate mousse and cranberry-raspberry purée.

More than anything else, cake-making of this type is an art form, a chance for each cook to show off his or her technique and creativity. The recipes in this chapter—in fact, throughout the book—are intended to give you a start, to inspire you, whether you want to make a dessert to dazzle dinner guests, or just to satisfy the artist in you.

Cranberry Christmas Cake

10 to 12 servings

Candied Cranberries
3 cups cranberries
1¼ cups sugar
¾ cup water

Chocolate Génoise
4 eggs
⅔ cup sugar
½ cup sifted cake flour
½ cup sifted unsweetened cocoa powder
3 tablespoons warm clarified butter
1 teaspoon vanilla

3 tablespoons Cointreau, Curacao or Grand Marnier

Chocolate Crème Fraîche
5 ounces bittersweet (not unsweetened) or semisweet chocolate, chopped
3 tablespoons water
5¼ cups well-chilled Crème Fraîche*

½ cup sugar
1 tablespoon vanilla
Chocolate curls

For cranberries: Place cranberries in heatproof bowl. Cook sugar and water in heavy small saucepan over low heat, swirling pan occasionally, until sugar dissolves. Increase heat and bring to boil. Pour boiling syrup over berries. Weight berries with plate. Bring water to boil in base of steamer. Place bowl on steamer rack. Cover and steam berries 45 minutes. Let stand at room temperature 3 to 4 days; do not stir.

For génoise: Preheat oven to 350°F. Grease 8x2-inch round cake pan; dust with flour. Combine eggs and sugar in bowl of electric mixer set over pan of barely simmering water. Heat the eggs to lukewarm, stirring occasionally. Transfer bowl to electric mixer and beat until eggs are cool and tripled in volume. Sift flour and cocoa together. Sift ⅓ of flour mixture over eggs and fold in gently. Repeat in 2 more additions. Transfer 1 cup batter to small bowl. Fold in butter and vanilla. Gently fold into remaining batter. Turn batter into prepared pan. Bake until cake begins to pull away from sides of pan and is springy, about 30 minutes. Cool in pan on rack.

Drain cranberries, reserving 3 tablespoons syrup. Combine reserved syrup with 3 tablespoons Cointreau.

For chocolate crème fraîche: Melt chocolate with water in top of double boiler set over barely simmering water, stirring until smooth. Cool. Beat ½ cup Crème Fraîche until soft peaks form. Fold into melted chocolate.

Beat remaining Crème Fraîche with sugar and vanilla until soft peaks form. Cut génoise into 3 layers using serrated knife. Place 1 layer cut side up on 8-inch-diameter cardboard round or platter. Brush with some of cranberry syrup. Spread all of chocolate crème fraîche over. Brush one side of center layer with syrup and arrange moist side down atop chocolate crème fraîche. Spread 2½ cups berries over cake, reserving remainder for garnish. Spread generous ½ cup whipped Crème Fraîche over berries. Brush cut side of last cake layer with syrup and set moist side down atop Crème Fraîche, pressing to compact layers. Brush top with remaining syrup. Spread some Crème Fraîche over top and sides of cake. Transfer remaining Crème Fraîche to pastry bag fitted with medium star tip. Pipe 12 to 14 rosettes around top edge of cake. Garnish with reserved candied cranberries and chocolate curls. Refrigerate cake at least 1 hour before serving.

*Crème Fraîche

Makes about 5¼ cups

5 cups whipping cream (preferably not ultrapasteurized)

5 tablespoons buttermilk

Heat cream in heavy small saucepan to lukewarm (85°F). Remove from heat and mix in buttermilk. Cover and let stand in warm draft-free area until slightly thickened, 24 to 48 hours, depending on temperature of room. Cover and refrigerate until ready to use. *(Can be prepared 2 days ahead.)*

Hazelnut Génoise with Fresh Cranberry Curd

12 servings

6 eggs, room temperature	¾ cup water
½ cup sugar	⅓ cup sugar
1 cup cake flour, sifted	⅓ cup kirsch
1½ cups unhusked hazelnuts, lightly toasted and finely minced	
1 teaspoon vanilla	Fresh Cranberry Curd*
¼ cup (½ stick) unsalted butter, clarified	1 cup whipping cream

Position rack in center of oven and preheat to 350°F. Line 12x18-inch jelly roll pan with parchment or waxed paper; butter and flour paper. Using electric mixer, beat eggs until well blended in bowl set over pot of warm water over low heat. Beat in ½ cup sugar 2 tablespoons at a time, then continue beating until egg mixture is pale and thick, about 10 minutes. Remove bowl from over water and beat until mixture triples in volume and forms slowly dissolving ribbon when beaters are lifted, about 12 minutes. Sift ¼ cup flour over egg mixture and fold in gently. Repeat with remaining flour in 3 additions. Fold in ⅓ cup hazelnuts.

Stir vanilla into butter. Fold butter into batter. Pour into prepared pan. Bake cake until springy and light brown, about 18 minutes. Invert onto rack; remove paper. Cool completely. Wrap and refrigerate overnight or freeze up to 3 months.

Heat water and ⅓ cup sugar in heavy small saucepan over low heat until sugar dissolves, swirling pan occasionally. Increase heat and bring to boil. Cool syrup to room temperature. Stir in kirsch. *(Can be prepared 1 week ahead, refrigerated.)*

Trim sides of cake. Brush top lightly with syrup. (Reserve remaining syrup for another use.) Using long serrated knife, cut cake lengthwise into 3 layers. Set 1 cake layer on platter. Spread with ½ cup cranberry curd. Top with second cake layer. Spread with ½ cup curd. Top with third cake layer. Spread with ½ cup curd.

Beat cream to stiff peaks. Fold in remaining curd. Reserve ¾ cup curd mixture. Spread remainder onto sides of cake. Press remaining hazelnuts onto sides of cake. Spoon reserved curd mixture into pastry bag fitted with small star tip. Pipe rosettes around top and bottom edges of cake. Pipe 3 rows of rosettes diagonally across top of cake. *(Can be prepared up to 12 hours ahead and refrigerated. Bring to room temperature before serving.)*

*Fresh Cranberry Curd

Makes about 2 cups

3½ cups cranberries	Pinch of salt
1 cup sugar	½ cup (1 stick) unsalted butter, melted and boiling hot
5 egg yolks	2 tablespoons kirsch
1 tablespoon fresh lemon juice	

Cook cranberries with ½ cup sugar in heavy medium saucepan over low heat until berries are very soft, stirring frequently, about 15 minutes.

Puree cranberries in processor. Press through fine strainer. Return to processor. Add yolks, remaining ½ cup sugar, lemon juice and salt and mix to combine. Blend in butter. Return to saucepan and stir over low heat until mixture is very thick and registers 170°F on candy thermometer, 10 to 12 minutes. Cool completely. Refrigerate at least 3 hours. *(Can be prepared 1 month ahead and refrigerated.)* Stir in 2 tablespoons kirsch just before using.

Spring Celebration Cake

8 to 10 servings

Génoise:
- 6 eggs, room temperature
- ¾ cup sugar
- 1 teaspoon vanilla
- 1½ teaspoons grated lemon peel
- 1 cup all purpose flour
- 5 tablespoons unsalted butter, melted and cooled to lukewarm

Chocolate Rum Buttercream
- 2½ cups powdered sugar
- 6 extra-large egg whites
- 1½ cups (3 sticks) unsalted butter, room temperature
- ¼ cup dark rum
- 1 teaspoon vanilla

- 1½ ounces semisweet chocolate, melted
- 2 pints fresh strawberries, hulled and sliced (reserve about 12 whole berries for garnish)

Whipped Cream Frosting
- 2 cups (1 pint) whipping cream, well chilled
- ¼ cup sifted powdered sugar
- 1 to 2 tablespoons dark rum (optional)
- 1 teaspoon vanilla
  Shelled and husked pistachios (garnish)

For génoise: Position rack in center of oven and preheat to 350°F. Grease bottoms of two 8-inch square pans (do not use nonstick pans). Line bottoms with parchment. Combine eggs, sugar and vanilla in large bowl of electric mixer. Whisk over pot of barely simmering water until mixture is warm to touch. Remove from heat, add lemon peel and beat at high speed until cooled to room temperature, tripled in volume and mixture forms slowly dissolving ribbon when beaters are lifted, 5 to 6 minutes. Sift flour over egg mixture in 6 additions, folding as gently as possible with rubber spatula after each addition. Gradually fold in butter, taking care to scrape bottom and sides of bowl with spatula. Divide batter evenly between prepared pans. Set pans on baking sheet. Bake until top of cake springs back when lightly touched and edges of cake pull away from pan, about 22 to 25 minutes. Cool on racks 5 minutes, then turn layers out onto racks to cool completely. Discard parchment.

For buttercream: Combine powdered sugar and whites in large metal bowl of electric mixer. Whisk directly over very low heat until mixture is warm and thick, about 5 to 7 minutes. Remove from heat and beat at high speed until cooled to room temperature (mixture will be very thick and fluffy). Cream butter in another large bowl until light and fluffy. Gradually beat egg white mixture into butter at medium speed. Beat in rum and vanilla. Divide buttercream in half. Blend melted chocolate into 1 half of buttercream.

Cut cake layers in half vertically to form four 4x8-inch rectangles. Split each rectangle horizontally to form 8 thinner 4x8-inch rectangles. Place 1 cake rectangle crosswise on center of 24-inch-long sheet of foil. Spread with ¼ of chocolate buttercream. Top with second cake layer. Spread with thin layer of plain buttercream.

Arrange single layer of sliced strawberries on buttercream. Spread with second thin layer of plain buttercream. Set third cake layer atop strawberry and buttercream layer, pressing gently. Spread with ¼ of chocolate buttercream. Continue alternating cake and buttercream, alternating chocolate and strawberry for total of 4 chocolate and 3 strawberry layers; reserve any remaining sliced strawberries for garnish. Top with final cake layer. Bring long ends of foil up against cake and over top, smoothing against sides and evening layers as much as possible. Insert 2 long skewers into cake to stabilize layers until buttercream sets. Chill until buttercream is firm, at least 2 hours.

About 1 or 2 hours before serving, remove cake from refrigerator. Discard skewers and foil. Carefully turn cake on its side on large platter (layers will be vertical, with cake resting on long edges). Tidy edges of cake with knife.

For frosting: Just before serving, combine cream and powdered sugar in large bowl and whip until stiff peaks form. Blend in rum and vanilla. Cover cake with whipped cream frosting. Garnish with pistachios and reserved sliced and whole strawberries. To serve, cut slices perpendicular to layers so that each slice reveals all 8 layers.

Chocolate Pecan Torte with Strawberry Buttercream

Brownielike layers are filled with a wonderful buttercream and glazed.

14 to 16 servings

Butter
¾ cup (1½ sticks) unsalted butter, room temperature
2 cups sugar
8 eggs
2 tablespoons vanilla
¼ teaspoon salt
12 ounces imported bittersweet or semisweet chocolate, melted

3½ cups pecan halves, very finely ground

Strawberry Buttercream*

Easy Chocolate Glaze**
7 to 8 medium strawberries (unhulled), halved lengthwise

Preheat oven to 375°F. Butter four 9-inch round cake pans. Line bottoms with parchment; butter parchment. Using electric mixer, cream ¾ cup butter until light. Add sugar and beat until light and fluffy. Beat in eggs one at a time. Add vanilla and salt. Using rubber spatula, stir in chocolate, then pecans. Divide batter among prepared pans. Bake until tester inserted in center comes out fudgy but not wet, about 22 minutes (top may crack). Cool in pans on racks 5 minutes. Run knife around edge of cakes. Invert onto racks. Discard parchment. Cool layers completely. *(Can be prepared up to 2 days ahead. Wrap each layer separately with plastic and refrigerate.)*

Arrange one cake layer bottom side up on platter. Slide strips of waxed paper under cake (this will keep platter neat during glazing). Spread ⅔ cup Strawberry Buttercream over layer. Repeat with remaining layers and buttercream, ending with cake bottom side up. Pat layers to even. Cover and refrigerate torte for at least 6 hours.

Cut edges of cake with serrated knife to even if necessary. Pour glaze over cake; smooth over sides and top. Discard waxed paper. *(Can be prepared 1 day ahead and refrigerated.)* Arrange strawberries around top edge of torte, cut side down. Let stand at room temperature 1 hour before serving.

*Strawberry Buttercream

Makes about 2½ cups

1¼ cups (2½ sticks) unsalted butter, cut into tablespoons and softened slightly
2 cups powdered sugar, sifted

4 egg yolks
½ cup pureed fresh strawberries
3 tablespoons strawberry preserves

Using electric mixer, cream butter and sugar until light and fluffy. Mix in yolks, then pureed berries and preserves. Cover tightly and refrigerate until set. *(Can be prepared 2 days ahead.)* Soften buttercream at room temperature until spreadable.

**Easy Chocolate Glaze

Makes about 2 cups

3 ounces semisweet chocolate, coarsely chopped
½ cup water
6 tablespoons (¾ stick) unsalted butter

3 tablespoons safflower oil
¾ cup unsweetened cocoa powder
½ cup plus 2 tablespoons sugar

Heat chocolate, water, butter and oil in top of double boiler over gently simmering water until chocolate melts. Remove from heat. Add cocoa powder and sugar and stir until sugar dissolves and glaze is smooth. Let cool until glaze is thickened slightly but still pourable.

Triple Mocha Square

With coffee in the cake, filling and buttercream frosting, this dessert is sure to be popular with mocha lovers.

16 servings

Mocha Cake
¼ cup boiling water
2 tablespoons instant espresso powder
1 cup all purpose flour
1 teaspoon baking powder

3 eggs, room temperature, separated
1 cup sugar
¼ teaspoon cream of tartar

Chocolate Mocha Filling
3½ ounces semisweet chocolate, broken into small pieces
2 tablespoons coffee liqueur
5 tablespoons unsalted butter, cut into pieces

Mocha Buttercream
2 tablespoons instant espresso powder
2 teaspoons boiling water
1 cup (2 sticks) unsalted butter, cut into ¼-inch slices

2 eggs
6 tablespoons sugar

Chocolate coffee bean candies (garnish)

For cake: Preheat oven to 300°F. Butter and flour 9x12-inch cake pan. Combine water and espresso powder in small bowl and set aside. Sift flour with baking powder in another bowl and set aside.

Beat egg yolks in large bowl until thick and pale yellow. Gradually add sugar, beating constantly. Stir in flour mixture. Blend in espresso. Beat egg whites in another bowl with cream of tartar until stiff and glossy. Carefully fold into yolk mixture.

Pour batter into prepared pan, spreading evenly. Bake until edges of cake shrink slightly from pan and tester inserted in center comes out clean, about 25 to 30 minutes. Remove cake from pan and let cool on wire rack.

For filling: Combine chocolate and coffee liqueur in top of double boiler and melt over hot (not boiling) water, stirring occasionally until smooth. Remove from heat. Add butter one piece at a time and beat with wooden spoon until mixture is consistency of mayonnaise. If not thick enough, set in bowl of ice water and beat to proper consistency, about 1 to 2 minutes.

For buttercream: Combine espresso powder and boiling water in small bowl and stir until dissolved. Set aside. Cream butter in another bowl until soft and fluffy.

Beat eggs in top of double boiler. Add sugar and beat until thick and pale yellow. Place over simmering water and cook, beating constantly with electric mixer at medium-high speed until thick and creamy, about 4 minutes. Transfer to bowl. Blend in espressso. Gradually add butter, beating constantly. Continue beating until mixture is cool, thick, glossy and slightly lightened in color, 3 to 5 minutes.

To assemble: Slice cake crosswise into 2 sections using serrated knife. Carefully split each section horizontally, making 4 layers. Reserve top layer. Spread filling thinly and evenly over remaining 3 layers. Stack layers on serving platter filling side up, topping with reserved unfilled layer cut side down.

Spread half of buttercream over top and sides of cake. Spoon remainder into pastry bag filled with decorative tip. Pipe rosettes around rim and several over top. Place chocolate coffee beans in centers of rosettes. Refrigerate until 1 hour before serving. To serve, cut crosswise into strips and cut each strip in half through center.

Mocha Pecan Pavé

8 to 10 servings

Sponge Cake
- 1 cup pecans, toasted
- 1½ cups all purpose flour
- 8 eggs, room temperature
- 1½ cups sugar
- 1 teaspoon vanilla
- ¼ teaspoon almond extract

Buttercream
- ¾ cup sugar
- ⅓ cup water
- ¼ teaspoon fresh lemon juice
- 6 egg yolks, room temperature
- 1½ cups (3 sticks) unsalted butter, cut into tablespoon-size pieces, room temperature

- 3 tablespoons instant coffee powder
- 2 tablespoons hot brewed coffee
- 3 ounces semisweet chocolate, melted and cooled

Rum Syrup
- ½ cup water
- ¼ cup sugar
- Dash of fresh lemon juice
- 3 tablespoons dark rum

Ganache
- 8 ounces semisweet chocolate
- 1 cup whipping cream

- Ground toasted pecans
- Chocolate coffee bean candies

For cake: Preheat oven to 350°F. Line 12x18-inch baking pan with parchment, allowing 2-inch overhang. Butter and flour paper. Grind pecans with 2 tablespoons flour in processor. Transfer to bowl. Add remaining flour and mix well. Beat eggs and sugar in large bowl of electric mixer until slowly dissolving ribbon forms when beaters are lifted. Blend in vanilla and almond extract. Fold in flour mixture in 3 additions. Turn batter into prepared pan, spreading evenly. Bake until tester inserted in center comes out clean, about 10 minutes. Invert cake onto rack. Remove paper. Cool completely. *(Can be prepared 2 days ahead. Store in airtight container.)*

For buttercream: Heat sugar, water and lemon juice in heavy small saucepan over low heat until sugar dissolves, swirling pan occasionally. Increase heat and boil sugar syrup until candy thermometer registers 239°F (soft-ball stage). Blend yolks at medium speed in large bowl of electric mixer. Gradually beat syrup into yolks in thin stream and continue beating until completely cool. Beat in butter 1 tablespoon at a time. Divide buttercream in half. Set aside.

Blend coffee powder and hot coffee. Cool completely. Add 1½ tablespoons cooled coffee mixture to half of buttercream. Add remaining coffee mixture and melted chocolate to remaining buttercream. *(Can be prepared 2 days ahead; chill.)*

For syrup: Heat water, sugar and lemon juice in heavy small saucepan over low heat until sugar dissolves, swirling pan occasionally. Increase heat and boil 1 minute. Cool completely. Add rum. *(Can be prepared 3 weeks ahead and refrigerated.)*

For ganache: Coarsely chop chocolate in processor. Bring cream just to boil. With machine running, pour hot cream through feed tube and mix until chocolate melts. Pour ganache into bowl. Let stand at room temperature until thickened.

To assemble: Split cake into 2 layers. Cut each in half crosswise. Brush each piece lightly with rum syrup (reserve remainder for another use). Set 1 cake layer on platter. Spread with half of ganache. Top with second cake layer. Spread with half of coffee buttercream. Top with third cake layer. Spread with remaining ganache. Top with remaining cake layer. Refrigerate until set. Trim edges. Frost cake with coffee-chocolate buttercream. Press ground pecans onto sides of cake. Spoon remaining coffee buttercream into pastry bag fitted with star tip. Pipe rosettes over top of cake. Place chocolate coffee bean atop each rosette.

Gâteau Royale

Raspberry jam and almond paste complement the chocolate in this rich dessert.

10 servings

5 ounces semisweet or bittersweet (not unsweetened) chocolate, finely chopped
¼ cup (½ stick) unsalted butter, cut into pieces
3 tablespoons water
3 eggs, separated, room temperature
¾ cup sugar

¾ cup sifted cake flour
⅛ teaspoon cream of tartar
Pinch of salt

½ cup raspberry preserves
5 ounces almond paste
Chocolate Glaze*

Preheat oven to 350°F. Line base of 9-inch-diameter cake pan with parchment or waxed paper. Melt chocolate and butter with water in top of double boiler over barely simmering water, stirring until smooth. Remove from over water. Using electric mixer, beat yolks and ½ cup sugar until slowly dissolving ribbon forms when beaters are lifted. Mix in warm chocolate, then flour. Using clean, dry beater, beat whites with cream of tartar and salt until soft peaks form. Add remaining ¼ cup sugar 1 tablespoon at a time and beat until stiff but not dry. Gently fold ¼ of whites into batter to lighten; fold in remaining whites. Turn batter into prepared pan. Bake until tester inserted in center of cake comes out clean, 20 to 25 minutes. Cool cake in pan 10 minutes. Invert onto rack, discarding paper, and cool completely. *(Can be prepared 1 day ahead. Wrap tightly and store at room temperature.)*

Using serrated knife, cut cake into 2 layers. Arrange 1 layer cut surface up on 9-inch cardboard round. Spread with half of preserves. Top with second layer, cut side down. Spread with remaining preserves. Roll almond paste between sheets of plastic wrap to thickness of ⅛ inch. Cut out 9-inch circle, using cake pan as guide. Place circle atop cake. Spread cake sides with just enough glaze to smooth out any imperfections; be careful to keep crumbs out of remaining glaze. Gently reheat remaining glaze over barely simmering water until smooth and just pourable but not thin and watery. Strain glaze through fine sieve. Place cake on bakery turntable or plate. Reserve 3 tablespoons glaze; pour remainder onto center of cake. Using clean metal spatula, spread over top and sides of cake, working glaze as little as possible. Let stand 5 minutes. Spoon reserved glaze into parchment cone with small opening. Pipe decoratively atop cake. Transfer cake to rack. Let stand until glaze is set. Serve at room temperature.

*Chocolate Glaze

Makes about 1¼ cups

½ cup (1 stick) unsalted butter, cut into small pieces
6 ounces semisweet or bittersweet (not unsweetened) chocolate, finely chopped

1 tablespoon corn syrup

Melt butter and chocolate with corn syrup in double boiler over barely simmering water, stirring until smooth. Cool until almost set but still spreadable.

Celestial Almond Cream Cake

Make this heavenly dessert the same day you serve it.

8 to 10 servings

Almond Cream
1 envelope unflavored gelatin
5 tablespoons cold water

4 egg whites, room temperature
½ cup sugar
½ teaspoon vanilla
½ teaspoon almond extract
½ cup whipping cream, beaten to soft peaks
1 8-inch Amaretto Cake* layer

Custard Sauce
2 cups milk
1 tablespoon cornstarch

½ cup sugar
4 egg yolks, room temperature
½ teaspoon vanilla
½ teaspoon almond extract

1 10-ounce package frozen raspberries, thawed (reserve juice)
⅔ cup blanched slivered almonds, lightly toasted

For cream: Sprinkle gelatin over water in small bowl. Set in pan of simmering water and stir until dissolved. Cool.

Lightly oil sides of 8½-inch springform pan. Using electric mixer, beat whites to soft peaks. Gradually add sugar and beat until stiff and shiny. Gently whisk in cooled gelatin mixture, vanilla and almond extract. Fold in whipped cream. Fit cake layer into bottom of prepared pan. Pour almond cream over cake. Cover with plastic wrap. Chill several hours to firm.

For sauce: Blend ½ cup milk and cornstarch in heavy medium saucepan. Gradually whisk in remaining milk and sugar. Set over medium heat and stir until mixture coats back of spoon, about 10 minutes. Whisk some of milk mixture into yolks. Whisk back into milk mixture and stir until slightly thickened and smooth, about 2 minutes. Pour into bowl. Stir in vanilla and almond extract. Cool completely. Cover and chill until ready to serve.

Puree raspberries and juice in blender or processor. Strain through fine sieve to eliminate seeds. Cover and refrigerate until ready to serve.

Pour ¾ of raspberry puree on platter. Remove springform from cake. Using long spatula, lift cake from bottom of pan and set in center of platter. Pour half of sauce over. Sprinkle with almonds. Cut into wedges and serve. Pass remaining raspberry puree and sauce separately.

*Pound or sponge cake can be substituted.

*Amaretto Cake

If serving this cake on its own, bake it in a bundt pan. Sprinkle the top with slivered almonds before baking, then dust with powdered sugar before using. Fresh fruit makes a delicious accompaniment.

8 servings

2½ cups sifted bleached all purpose flour
1 tablespoon baking powder
¼ teaspoon salt
½ cup amaretto liqueur
½ cup milk, room temperature
1 teaspoon vanilla
½ teaspoon almond extract
1 cup (2 sticks) unsalted butter, room temperature
1¾ cups sugar
4 eggs, room temperature

Preheat oven to 350°F. Grease 1 bundt pan or three 8-inch round cake pans. Line cake pans with parchment paper; grease paper. Sift flour, baking powder and salt into bowl. Blend amaretto, milk, vanilla and almond extract in another bowl. Using electric mixer, beat butter until light. Gradually add sugar and beat until light and fluffy. Beat in eggs 1 at a time. Fold in flour mixture and liquid alternately in 3 additions, starting and ending with flour mixture; do not overblend. Pour into prepared pans. Bake until cake is golden brown and pulls away from sides of pan, 25 to 30 minutes for cake pans and 55 to 60 minutes for bundt pan. Cool cake completely in pan on rack. *(Can be prepared 1 day ahead and stored at room temperature.)*

Princess Cake

This beautiful marzipan-wrapped cake is perfect for special occasions.

8 to 10 servings

Custard Filling
1¼ cups half and half
2 eggs, room temperature
⅓ cup plus 1 tablespoon sugar
¼ cup all purpose flour
2 tablespoons (¼ stick) unsalted butter
2 teaspoons vanilla

Marzipan Topping
11 ounces almond paste, crumbled
1⅓ cups powdered sugar (or more), sifted
1 teaspoon almond extract
5 drops of green food coloring

Cake
4 eggs, room temperature
¾ cup plus 1 tablespoon sugar
⅓ cup plus 1 tablespoon unbleached all purpose flour
⅓ cup plus 1 tablespoon potato flour
1 teaspoon baking powder

2 teaspoons unflavored gelatin
2 tablespoons cold water
⅔ cup well-chilled whipping cream
⅓ cup raspberry jam

Powdered sugar
Almond Paste Rose*

For filling: Scale half and half in heavy medium saucepan. Whisk eggs, sugar and flour in medium bowl. Gradually whisk in hot half and half. Return mixture to saucepan. Stir over low heat until custard thickens and leaves path on back of spoon when finger is drawn across, about 8 minutes; *do not boil.* Remove from heat and whisk in butter and vanilla. Transfer custard to medium bowl. Cool completely, stirring occasionally. *(Can be prepared 2 days ahead and refrigerated.)*

For marzipan: Blend almond paste and 1⅓ cups powdered sugar in processor until crumbly. With machine running, add almond extract and coloring through feed tube and process until well blended. Knead on work surface until green color is evenly distributed, adding more powdered sugar if sticky. Shape into ball; flatten to disc. *(Can be prepared 1 day ahead. Wrap in plastic and store at room temperature.)*

For cake: Position rack in lower third of oven and preheat to 350°F. Butter and flour 9-inch springform pan. Using electric mixer, beat eggs and sugar until pale yellow and slowly dissolving ribbon forms when beaters are lifted. Sift both flours and baking powder together. Gently fold into egg mixture 3 tablespoons at a time. Pour batter into prepared pan. Bake until tester inserted in center comes out clean, 25 to 30 minutes. Cool in pan on rack 10 minutes. Remove pan sides and cool cake completely; cake will fall. *(Can be prepared 1 day ahead. Wrap tightly.)*

To assemble: Sprinkle gelatin over 2 tablespoons cold water in small bowl; let soften 5 minutes. Set bowl in pan of simmering water and stir until gelatin dissolves. Whip cream until soft peaks form. Gradually add gelatin, mixing until stiff peaks form. Fold into filling. Run knife between cake and pan bottom and remove pan. Cut cake into 2 layers, using serrated knife. Place bottom layer on serving platter. Spread jam over, leave ¼-inch border. Top with a little less than ½ of filling. Add second cake layer, top with remaining filling, mounding slightly in center. Refrigerate 1½ hours.

Roll marzipan out between sheets of parchment or waxed paper to 13-inch-diameter round. Remove 1 sheet of paper. Using bottom sheet as aid, turn marzipan out onto cake; remove second sheet of paper. Gently wrap marzipan around cake. Trim edges. Refrigerate cake at least 1 hour. *(Can be prepared 6 hours ahead.)* Just before serving, sift powdered sugar over top of cake and place rose in center.

*Almond Paste Rose

Makes 1

1½ ounces almond paste
2 tablespoons powdered sugar

1 drop of red food coloring

Knead all ingredients together in small bowl until pale pink. Roll into 1x1½-inch oval log. Cut into eight ⅛-inch-thick slices. Pinch edges to flatten to 2¼x1½-inch ovals. Roll 1 oval up lengthwise into cylinder. Wrap second oval around cylinder. Pinch at base to seal. Repeat with remaining ovals, overlapping slightly. Open top of rose by curling petals back slightly. Cut base to flatten. *(Can be prepared up to 2 days ahead. Store rose in airtight container.)*

Molasses Stack Cake with Custard Sauce

12 to 16 servings

Molasses Cake
3½ cups all purpose flour
2 teaspoons baking powder
½ teaspoon baking soda
½ teaspoon salt

¾ cup (1½ sticks) butter or margarine, room temperature
½ cup sugar
1 cup unsulphured molasses
3 eggs, room temperature, well beaten
1 cup buttermilk

Apple Filling
8 or 9 tart apples (about 3 pounds total), cut into eighths, unpeeled, uncored
1 cup water
¼ cup unsulphured molasses

1 teaspoon cinnamon
1 teaspoon ginger
1 teaspoon grated lemon peel
Sugar (optional)

Custard Sauce
1 cup milk
3 marshmallows
2 tablespoons sugar
1½ teaspoons butter
1 teaspoon vanilla
Dash of salt

2 egg yolks
4½ teaspoons cornstarch
1 tablespoon Calvados
¼ teaspoon freshly grated nutmeg
½ cup whipping cream, whipped

Whipped cream (garnish)
Freshly grated nutmeg

For cake: Preheat oven to 350°F. Butter three 9-inch round pans. Sift flour, baking powder, baking soda and salt.

Cream butter in medium bowl. Gradually blend in sugar, beating until light and fluffy. Add molasses and mix thoroughly. Gradually beat in eggs. Add sifted dry ingredients and buttermilk alternately to molasses mixture, blending well; do not overbeat.

Divide batter among prepared cake pans, spreading evenly. Bake until tester inserted in center comes out clean, about 25 to 30 minutes (layers will be thin, about ¾ to 1 inch high). Run sharp knife around edges of cake layers. Cool on racks.

For filling: Combine apples and water in large saucepan and bring to boil over medium-high heat. Reduce heat to very low, cover and simmer, stirring frequently, until apples are tender when pierced, about 20 to 25 minutes.

Transfer apples to food mill using medium disc or press through coarse sieve with spoon. Discard peels, cores and seeds. Transfer applesauce to saucepan. Add molasses, cinnamon, ginger and grated lemon peel and cook over medium heat, stirring occasionally, until thick, about 8 to 10 minutes. Taste and add sugar if desired.

For sauce: Combine milk, marshmallows, sugar, butter, vanilla and salt in top of double boiler. Place over simmering water and cook until mixture is hot and marshmallows have melted.

Combine egg yolks and cornstarch in small bowl and beat well. Pour ½ cup hot milk mixture into yolks, stirring rapidly. Return yolk mixture to double boiler and cook sauce until thick and creamy, stirring constantly, about 5 minutes. Remove from heat. Add Calvados and nutmeg. Turn into bowl. Cool completely. Gently fold in whipped cream. Cover and refrigerate until 30 minutes before serving.

To assemble: Using serrated knife, cut each cake horizontally into 2 layers. Reserve top layer. Spread apple filling evenly over cut side of remaining 5 layers. Stack layers on serving platter filling side up, topping with reserved layer cut side down. Mound whipped cream in center and sprinkle with nutmeg. Serve with custard sauce.

Lundi Gras Chocolate Cake

There are two simple tricks to preparing this fancy dessert. First, be certain to use almond paste, not marzipan. Second, when making the filling, fold the unwhipped cream into the melted chocolate gently; do not beat.

12 servings

Cake

    9 eggs, separated, room temperature
    ¾ cup sugar
    1 tablespoon vanilla
       Pinch of salt
    ¼ teaspoon cream of tartar
    ¾ cup unsweetened cocoa powder

   14 ounces almond paste
    1 to 2 tablespoons amaretto liqueur
       (optional)

       Powdered sugar

    ¾ cup amaretto liqueur

Chocolate Filling

   27 ounces extra-bittersweet or
       bittersweet chocolate, chopped
    3 tablespoons unsalted butter
    1 quart whipping cream, room
       temperature

    2 cups whipping cream, whipped

For cake: Preheat oven to 350°F. Line 10x15x1-inch jelly roll pan with parchment; butter parchment. Beat yolks, ¾ cup sugar, vanilla and salt with electric mixer until pale yellow and slowly dissolving ribbon forms when beaters are lifted. Beat whites with cream of tartar in another large bowl until soft peaks form. Fold ⅓ of whites into yolks to lighten; spoon remaining whites atop yolks. Sift on cocoa and fold until just combined. Spread in prepared pan. Bake until springy to touch, about 25 minutes.

Meanwhile, if almond paste is dry or crumbly, combine in processor with 1 tablespoon amaretto. Blend until soft enough to roll out, adding more amaretto by teaspoons if necessary. Roll almond paste out between 2 sheets of waxed paper into 9x14-inch rectangle. Refrigerate.

Dust kitchen towel with powdered sugar. Turn cake out onto towel; remove paper. Trim ½ inch off edges of cake. Place almond paste on hot cake. Roll cake up jelly roll fashion, starting at one long side. Cool completely.

Pour ¾ cup amaretto into pie plate. Cut cake into ⅓-inch-thick slices. Dip one side of each slice briefly into amaretto. Cover bottom of 10-inch springform pan with some of cake slices, dipped side down, working from edge to center and arranging open ends of slices facing in same direction. Press very firmly to secure slices. Place remaining slices upright against sides of pan; press firmly to secure. Refrigerate cake while preparing filling.

For filling: Melt chocolate and butter in top of double boiler over barely simmering water, stirring until smooth. Transfer to large bowl. Immediately add 1 quart cream in 3 additions, gently folding just until combined; do not beat. Pour into cake-lined pan. Cover and refrigerate overnight.

Cut edges of cake even with filling if necessary. Invert cake onto serving platter. Let stand at room temperature 20 minutes. Spoon whipped cream into pastry bag fitted with star tip. Pipe some cream decoratively around cake. Pass remaining cream separately with cake slices.

Chocolate Cream Cake

6 to 8 servings

Custard
- 1 cup half and half
- 1 vanilla bean, split

- 2 eggs, room temperature
- 2½ tablespoons sugar
- ½ cup orgeat syrup*

Cake
- 2 eggs, room temperature
- ½ cup sugar
- ½ teaspoon vanilla
- ½ cup sifted cake flour
- ¼ teaspoon baking powder
- Pinch of salt

Chocolate Cream
- 4 tablespoons Irish whiskey
- 9 ounces bittersweet or semisweet chocolate, coarsely chopped
- 3 tablespoons milk

- 1 cup well-chilled whipping cream
- 3 tablespoons sugar

- ¼ cup chopped pistachio nuts

For custard: Scald half and half with vanilla bean in saucepan. Cool slightly.

Beat eggs and sugar until pale and thick. Gradually whisk in half and half. Return to saucepan and stir over medium-low heat until mixture thickens enough to leave path when finger is drawn across spoon, about 10 minutes; do not boil. Strain into bowl. Cool to room temperature. Stir in orgeat syrup. Refrigerate until ready to use. *(Can be prepared 2 days ahead.)*

For cake: Preheat oven to 400°F. Grease jelly roll pan. Line with waxed paper; grease and flour paper. Using electric mixer, beat eggs, sugar and vanilla until tripled in volume, about 10 minutes. Sift dry ingredients into egg mixture and fold gently. Spread batter evenly in prepared pan. Bake until tester inserted in center comes out clean and cake shrinks in from sides slightly, about 8 minutes. Invert cake onto towel; remove pan. Cool cake completely. *(Can be prepared 1 day ahead. Wrap tightly in plastic; store at room temperature.)*

Remove waxed paper from bottom of cake. Trim cake edges. Cut cake into 2 long pieces to fit 8¾x3¼x3-inch loaf pan. Line bottom of pan with 1 piece. Set remaining piece of cake aside.

For cream: Boil whiskey in heavy small saucepan until reduced by half. Remove from heat. Stir in ¼ of chocolate and all of milk. Add remaining chocolate and stir until melted and smooth, placing pan over low heat if necessary. Cool to room temperature, stirring mixture once or twice.

Beat cream with sugar in large bowl until soft peaks form. Gently but thoroughly fold in chocolate mixture. Spoon chocolate cream into cake-lined pan, spreading evenly. Top with second piece of cake, pressing gently. Refrigerate cake for at least 8 and up to 24 hours.

To serve, invert cake onto platter. Using moistened carving knife, cut into thin slices. Cover plates with custard. Top with cake. Sprinkle with nuts.

*Also known as almond milk and sirop d'orgeat. Available at specialty foods stores and many liquor stores.

 *Mousse Cakes*

Chocolate Butterscotch Torte

16 servings

Crust

1 8½-ounce box chocolate wafer cookies, coarsely chopped
3 ounces bittersweet or extra bittersweet (not unsweetened) chocolate, coarsely chopped
¼ cup butterscotch chips
¾ cup walnuts, lightly toasted and chopped
½ cup (1 stick) unsalted butter, melted and cooled

Filling

6 ounces unsweetened chocolate, chopped
⅓ cup butterscotch chips

2½ cups firmly packed dark brown sugar
1 8-ounce package cream cheese, room temperature
1 teaspoon vanilla

6 egg yolks
½ cup (1 stick) unsalted butter, cut into 8 pieces

3 egg whites, room temperature
1 tablespoon powdered sugar
⅛ teaspoon cream of tartar
2 cups whipping cream, whipped
¾ cup walnuts, lightly toasted and chopped

Leaves

3 ounces bittersweet or extra bittersweet (not unsweetened) chocolate, chopped
½ cup butterscotch chips
½ teaspoon butter

16 camellia leaves

1 cup well-chilled whipping cream
1 tablespoon powdered sugar, sifted
1 teaspoon vanilla

For crust: Mix cookies, chocolate and butterscotch chips in processor 20 seconds. Transfer to large bowl. Stir in chopped walnuts and melted butter, tossing until well blended. Press mixture into bottom and up sides of 9½-inch springform pan. Refrigerate crust while preparing filling.

For filling: Melt 3 ounces chocolate in double boiler over simmering water. Stir in butterscotch chips until well blended. Add remaining 3 ounces chocolate, mixing until smooth. Remove from over water.

Combine sugar, cream cheese and vanilla in large bowl over simmering water. Using electric mixer, beat until creamy, about 5 minutes. Beat in yolks 1 at a time. Continue beating until sugar dissolves and mixture is slightly thickened and forms slowly dissolving ribbon when beaters are lifted, about 10 minutes. Remove bowl from over water. Blend in butter 1 piece at a time. Stir in chocolate mixture. Cool to room temperature, stirring often, about 30 minutes.

Using clean dry beaters, beat whites with powdered sugar and cream of tartar until stiff but not dry. Fold whipped cream and whites into chocolate alternately in 3 additions. Gently fold in walnuts. Spoon into crust. Smooth top with spatula. Refrigerate at least 6 hours or overnight.

For leaves: Melt chocolate in double boiler or small bowl over simmering water. Melt butterscotch chips in another bowl over simmering water. Stir ¼ teaspoon butter into chocolate. Cool to room temperature. Stir remaining ¼ teaspoon butter into butterscotch. Cool to room temperature.

Spread chocolate over veined side of 8 leaves, being careful not to drip on edges. Arrange on plate, chocolate side up. Freeze until just firm, about 10 minutes. Starting at stem end, gently peel leaf away from chocolate, freezing briefly if too soft to work. Repeat with butterscotch and remaining leaves. *(Can be prepared up to 1 week ahead. Wrap and refrigerate.)*

Let torte stand at room temperature 20 minutes before serving. Meanwhile, whip cream with powdered sugar and vanilla to stiff peaks. Spoon some of whipped cream into pastry bag fitted with large star tip. Arrange leaves in center of torte, alternating colors. Pipe whipped cream around edge. Pass remaining cream separately.

Chocolate Gold

A triple chocolate treat: chocolate cake, kirsch- and coffee-enhanced mousse filling and chocolate glaze.

12 servings

Cake
- 2 ounces semisweet chocolate, coarsely chopped
- 2 tablespoons water

- 2 jumbo eggs
- ¼ cup sugar
- ½ cup sifted all purpose flour, resifted

Filling
- 3 tablespoons butter, melted
- 2½ tablespoons chocolate cherry liqueur
- 2½ tablespoons kirsch
- 2 eggs, separated

- 1½ tablespoons firmly packed light brown sugar
- 1 teaspoon instant coffee powder
- 8 ounces semisweet chocolate, melted
- 1 cup whipping cream
  Pinch of cream of tartar
  Pinch of salt
- 2 tablespoons powdered sugar

Glaze
- 6 ounces semisweet chocolate, coarsely chopped
- ¼ cup (½ stick) butter
- 2 tablespoons vegetable oil

For cake: Melt chocolate with water in double boiler over gently simmering water; stir until smooth. Remove from over water and let cool to lukewarm.

Preheat oven to 350°F. Butter jelly roll pan. Line with parchment paper; butter paper. In large bowl set over pan of hot water, whisk eggs and sugar until warm to touch. Remove bowl from over water. Using electric mixer, beat until mixture triples in volume. Sift in ⅓ of flour and fold gently. Fold in half of melted chocolate. Sift in ⅓ of flour and fold gently. Fold in remaining melted chocolate. Sift and fold in remaining flour. Spread batter evenly on prepared pan. Bake until springy to touch, about 20 minutes. Cool cake.

Line work surface with parchment. Invert cake onto paper. Peel paper off bottom of cake. Cut out one 12x3-inch strip of cake; line bottom of 12x3-inch loaf pan. Cut out two 12x2-inch strips of cake; line sides of pan. Cut out two 3x2-inch pieces of cake; fit onto short ends of pan.

For filling: Blend butter, liqueur, kirsch, yolks, brown sugar and coffee in large bowl. Stir in melted chocolate. Using electric mixer, beat cream until soft peaks form. Fold into chocolate mixture. Using clean dry beaters, beat whites, cream of tartar and salt until soft peaks form. Gradually add powdered sugar and beat until stiff but not dry. Gently fold whites into filling. Spoon into cake-lined pan, smoothing evenly. Cover and refrigerate at least 3 hours. *(Can be prepared 1 week ahead.)*

For glaze: Melt chocolate and butter with oil in double boiler over gently simmering water; do not boil.

Invert cake onto platter. Drizzle glaze over top. Cut cake into thin slices.

Domed Chocolate Mousse Cake

After hollowing out the interior of the cake, reserve the pieces for use in a trifle, or crumble over ice cream.

8 to 12 servings

Cake
1½ cups sifted cake flour
1 cup unsweetened cocoa powder
Pinch of salt
12 eggs, separated
2 cups sugar
1 teaspoon vanilla
¼ teaspoon cream of tartar

Syrup
¾ cup water
½ cup sugar
2 tablespoons framboise (raspberry eau-de-vie)

Mousse
½ pound bittersweet or semisweet chocolate (preferably imported), coarsely chopped

1 egg, beaten to blend
2 eggs, separated, room temperature
1 tablespoon framboise
1 cup whipping cream

Ganache
2 cups whipping cream
1 pound bittersweet (not unsweetened) or semisweet chocolate (preferably imported), coarsely chopped

Raspberry Sauce
2 10-ounce packages frozen sweetened raspberries, thawed
1 cup fresh raspberries

For cake: Preheat oven to 350°F. Line 9-inch ovenproof bowl or colander with foil, allowing overhang. Generously butter foil. Sift flour, cocoa powder and salt into bowl. Beat yolks and 1¾ cups sugar in another bowl until thick and pale. Blend in vanilla. Gently whisk in half of dry ingredients. Using electric mixer, beat whites and cream of tartar until soft peaks form. Add remaining ¼ cup sugar 1 tablespoon at a time and beat until stiff but not dry. Gently fold ⅓ of whites into batter. Fold in remaining dry ingredients, then whites. Pour into foil-lined bowl. Bake 15 minutes. Reduce oven to 325°F. Continue baking until tester inserted in center comes out clean, about 50 minutes. Cool cake completely in bowl.

For syrup: Cook water and sugar in heavy small saucepan over low heat until sugar dissolves completely, swirling pan occasionally. Bring syrup to boil. Cool completely. Stir in framboise.

For mousse: Melt chocolate in large bowl set over pan of gently simmering water; stir until smooth. Remove bowl from over water. Whisk in egg. Whisk in yolks 1 at a time. Stir in framboise. Beat cream to medium-stiff peaks. Fold into chocolate mixture. Beat whites until stiff but not dry. Fold whites into melted chocolate mixture.

To assemble: Using foil overhang as handles, remove cake from bowl. Cut off 1-inch layer from flat side of cake and reserve. Return cake to bowl. Scoop out inside of cake, leaving 1-inch shell. Brush inside of cake with syrup. Fill with mousse. Brush reserved layer with syrup. Fit tightly over cake. Cover and refrigerate overnight.

For ganache: Heat cream in heavy medium saucepan. Remove from heat. Add chocolate and stir until smooth. Cool mixture until spreadable, stirring occasionally; do not let ganache set.

For sauce: Puree thawed raspberries in processor. Strain into bowl to remove seeds. Fold in fresh raspberries.

Invert cake onto platter. Peel off any foil; brush off crumbs. Frost cake with half of ganache. Spoon remaining ganache into pastry bag fitted with large star tip. Pipe rosettes around base of cake. Serve with raspberry sauce.

Raspberry Chocolate Mousse Cake

8 servings

Cake
- 2 small eggs, room temperature
- 5 tablespoons sugar
- 3 tablespoons all purpose flour
- 2 tablespoons unsweetened cocoa powder

Mousse
- 3 tablespoons sugar
- 3 tablespoons water
- 2 small egg yolks, room temperature
- 6 ounces semisweet chocolate, melted
- 1½ cups whipping cream, beaten to soft peaks
- 4 cups (or more) fresh raspberries

Syrup
- 2 tablespoons sugar
- 2 tablespoons water
- ¼ cup red currant jelly
- 8 ounces semisweet chocolate

For cake: Preheat oven to 350°F. Butter and flour 8-inch springform pan. Line bottom with parchment paper; butter and flour paper. Gently whisk eggs and sugar in bowl over low heat until warm to touch. Beat with electric mixer until cool and tripled in volume. Sift together flour and cocoa powder. Gradually and gently fold into egg mixture. Turn batter into prepared pan. Bake until cake shrinks from sides of pan and top springs back when lightly touched, about 25 minutes. Cool in pan 20 minutes. Run knife around sides. Remove springform. Cool cake. Clean springform.

For mousse: Heat sugar and water in heavy small saucepan over low heat until sugar dissolves, swirling pan occasionally. Increase heat and bring syrup to boil. Whisk yolks in large bowl. Using electric mixer, beat in syrup in thin stream. Continue beating until mixture cools and triples in volume. Beat in melted chocolate. Fold in whipped cream. Refrigerate if necessary until firm enough to pipe.

To assemble: Cut cake horizontally into 3 layers. Set 1 layer on base of springform pan. Attach springform. Spoon mousse into pastry bag fitted with plain tip. Pipe ½-inch layer of mousse over cake. Arrange 1 cup raspberries on top. Cover with second cake layer. Pipe ½-inch layer of mousse onto cake. Arrange 1 cup raspberries atop mousse. Top with third cake layer. Pipe ¼-inch layer of mousse onto cake. Refrigerate 30 minutes.

For syrup: Heat sugar and water in heavy small saucepan over low heat until sugar dissolves, swirling pan occasionally. Increase heat and bring to boil. Reduce heat, add currant jelly and stir until jelly has melted.

Cut 3x27-inch sheet of waxed paper. Wrap hot damp towel around springform. Remove springform. Melt 8 ounces chocolate in double boiler over gently simmering water. Stir until smooth. Spread ⅛-inch-thick layer of chocolate on waxed paper, covering completely. Let stand until set, 2 to 3 minutes. Leaving waxed paper attached, wrap chocolate band around cake, overlapping slightly to seal. Decorate top of cake with remaining 2 cups raspberries, adding more if necessary to cover completely. Brush raspberries generously with syrup. Carefully remove waxed paper from chocolate with thin paring knife.

Chocolate Cranberry Trifle Cake

8 servings

Chocolate Sponge Cake
    All purpose flour
½ cup all purpose flour
⅓ cup unsweetened cocoa powder
6 eggs, separated, room temperature
1 cup sugar
½ teaspoon vanilla

½ teaspoon cream of tartar
    Pinch of salt

Cranberry Filling
12 ounces fresh cranberries
1 cup sugar
1 tablespoon fresh lemon juice

Grand Marnier Sauce
1¼ cups milk
½ cup whipping cream
4 egg yolks

½ cup sugar
3 tablespoons Grand Marnier
1 teaspoon vanilla

Chocolate Mousse
1 teaspoon instant espresso powder
¼ cup boiling water
¾ cup sugar
4 ounces unsweetened chocolate, coarsely chopped
6 tablespoons (¾ stick) unsalted butter, cut into 6 pieces
4 eggs, separated, room temperature
1 teaspoon vanilla

    Pinch of salt
    Pinch of cream of tartar

½ cup finely chopped walnuts

For cake: Preheat oven to 325°F. Butter two 8-inch cake pans. Line with parchment; butter and flour paper, shaking off excess. Sift together ½ cup flour and cocoa powder. Using electric mixer, beat yolks and ½ cup sugar in large bowl until slowly dissolving ribbon forms when beaters are lifted. Blend in vanilla. Gradually beat in dry ingredients, stopping to scrape down sides of mixing bowl.

Using clean, dry beaters, beat whites, cream of tartar and salt until soft peaks form. Gradually add remaining sugar and beat until whites are stiff but not dry. Gently fold whites into batter in 2 additions. Pour batter into prepared pans. Bake until cake pulls away from sides of pan and top springs back when lightly touched, 25 to 30 minutes. Invert onto racks and cool completely. *(Can be prepared 2 days ahead. Wrap and store at room temperature.)*

For filling: Combine all ingredients in heavy medium saucepan and slowly bring to boil. Reduce heat and simmer 3 minutes. Set aside 15 large berries for decoration. Continue simmering remaining berries until mixture is jamlike, about 5 minutes. Cool completely. *(Can be prepared 3 days ahead.)*

For sauce: Heat milk and cream in heavy small saucepan until skin forms on top, about 5 minutes. Whisk yolks to blend in double boiler. Gradually whisk in sugar. Slowly stir in milk mixture. Set over gently simmering water and stir with wooden spoon until mixture thickens and finger leaves path when drawn across spoon, about 12 minutes. Cool completely. Blend in Grand Marnier and vanilla. Cover and refrigerate until ready to serve. *(Can be prepared 2 days ahead.)*

For mousse: Dissolve espresso powder in water in heavy small saucepan. Add ½ cup sugar and cook over low heat until sugar is dissolved, swirling pan occasionally. Bring to boil. Reduce heat to lowest setting. Add chocolate and stir until melted. Transfer to large bowl. Whisk in butter 1 piece at a time. Beat in yolks. Blend in vanilla.

Using clean, dry beaters, beat whites with salt and cream of tartar until soft peaks form. Gradually add remaining sugar and beat until whites are stiff but not dry. Stir ¼ of whites into chocolate mixture. Fold chocolate mixture into remaining whites. Cover and refrigerate until ready to use.

To assemble: Line edges of cake platter with 4 strips of waxed paper. Set 1 cake layer on platter. Spread with half of filling; do not let any run down sides. Spread with half of mousse. Sprinkle with half of walnuts. Repeat with remaining ingredients. Arrange reserved cranberries decoratively on top of cake. Cut sheet of waxed paper long enough to encircle cake. Fold paper in half lengthwise. Wrap around cake to support. Secure with string or tape. Refrigerate at least 2 hours to firm.

Bring cake to room temperature. Remove collar from cake and strips from platter. Cut cake into slices. Spoon several tablespoons of sauce onto each plate. Top with cake slice and serve.

White Wine Mousse Cake

A spectacular cake wrapped in marzipan and decorated with a marzipan grape cluster. Use a good-quality wine for the mousse.

10 servings

Cake
- 4 eggs, room temperature
- ½ cup sugar
- 1 cup all purpose flour

Syrup
- ¼ cup sugar
- ¼ cup water
- 1 teaspoon fresh lemon juice
- 2 tablespoons dry white wine

White Wine Mousse
- 1 teaspoon unflavored gelatin
- 2 tablespoons fresh lemon juice
- 2 egg yolks
- 6 tablespoons sugar
- ¼ cup dry white wine
- 1 cup plus 9 tablespoons well-chilled whipping cream
- 27 ounces marzipan
- 1 tablespoon (about) sifted unsweetened cocoa powder
  Yellow and green food coloring
- 2 ounces bittersweet (not unsweetened) or semisweet chocolate, melted

For cake: Preheat oven to 350°F. Butter 10-inch-diameter cake pan and dust with flour. Whisk eggs and sugar in heatproof bowl set over pan of simmering water until warm to touch, about 1 minute. Remove from heat. Beat eggs until tripled in volume. Sift flour over eggs in 4 additions, gently folding in until just combined; do not overmix. Pour batter into prepared pan. Bake until cake begins to pull away from sides of pan, about 25 minutes. Invert onto rack and cool completely. Wrap in plastic and chill until firm. *(Can be prepared 1 day ahead.)*

For syrup: Cook sugar, water and lemon juice in small saucepan over low heat, swirling pan occasionally, until sugar dissolves completely. Increase heat and bring syrup to boil. Cool. Mix in wine.

For mousse: Sprinkle gelatin over 1 tablespoon lemon juice in small bowl. Let soften 5 minutes. Place bowl in pan of simmering water and stir until gelatin dissolves. Beat yolks and sugar in medium bowl until light in color. Bring wine and remaining 1 tablespoon lemon juice to boil in heavy medium saucepan. Gradually whisk into yolks. Return to pan. Bring just to boil, stirring constantly. Remove from heat and mix in gelatin. Let stand until cooled to room temperature but not set, stirring frequently. Beat cream in medium bowl until soft peaks form. Fold ¼ of cream into egg mixture to lighten; fold in remaining cream.

To assemble: Cut cake into 2 layers, using serrated knife. Place 1 layer on 10-inch-diameter cardboard round, cut side up. Place on base of 10-inch springform pan or surround with 10-inch ring. Secure pan sides around cake. Brush cake with 1½ tablespoons syrup. Spread 1½ cups mousse over. Top with second layer, cut side down. Brush with 1½ tablespoons syrup. Spread remaining mousse evenly over, smoothing top. Refrigerate until mousse is set, at least 3 hours. *(Can be prepared 1 day ahead.)*

Roll 15 ounces marzipan out to ⅛-inch-thick round. Wrap warm damp kitchen towel around springform pan; gently release sides. Carefully drape marzipan over cake. Trim edges and tuck under cake. Knead enough cocoa powder into 2 ounces of marzipan to tint to color of bark. Form into grape branch. Knead enough yellow and green food coloring into 8 ounces of marzipan to tint to color of green grapes. Form by half-teaspoons into rounds for grapes. Knead enough green food coloring into remaining 2 ounces marzipan to tint leaf green. Roll out ⅛ inch thick and cut into leaf shapes. Arrange grapes, branches and leaves decoratively atop cake. Spoon melted chocolate into parchment cone with small opening. Pipe chocolate in thin line around upper edge of cake. *(Can be prepared 6 hours ahead and refrigerated. Let cake stand at room temperature for 20 minutes before serving.)*

Strawberry Mousse Cake

8 servings

Génoise

- 3 eggs, room temperature
- 9 tablespoons sugar
- 3 egg whites, room temperature
- ⅛ teaspoon cream of tartar
- 1 tablespoon plus 1½ teaspoons sugar
- ½ cup plus 1 tablespoon very finely ground almonds
- ¼ cup plus 1 teaspoon all purpose flour
- 1 tablespoon plus 1½ teaspoons butter, melted

Syrup

- ½ cup sugar
- ¼ cup water
- 1 tablespoon vodka
- 1 teaspoon fresh lemon juice

Strawberry Mousse

- 1 12-ounce bag individually frozen strawberries, thawed and drained (juice reserved)
- 2 teaspoons unflavored gelatin
- ¼ cup sugar
- 2 cups well-chilled whipping cream

- ½ pint strawberries, halved
  Red currant jelly, melted

For génoise: Preheat oven to 375°F. Place dabs of butter in corners of two 16x12-inch baking sheets. Line with parchment (butter will help hold in place). Whisk whole eggs and 9 tablespoons sugar in large bowl set over pan of simmering water until eggs are barely warm. Remove from over water. Using electric mixer, beat eggs until tripled in volume. Using clean dry beater, beat whites and cream of tartar in another bowl until soft peaks form. Add 1 tablespoon plus 1½ teaspoons sugar and beat until stiff but not dry. Gently fold whites into whole eggs. Gently fold in ground almonds, flour and butter. Spread 3 cups batter on each prepared pan to form ⅛-inch-thick layer. Bake until light brown and springy to touch, 15 to 20 minutes. Cool completely in pan.

For syrup: Cook sugar and water in heavy small saucepan over low heat, swirling pan occasionally, until sugar dissolves. Increase heat and bring to boil. Remove from heat and let cool. Mix in vodka and lemon juice.

For mousse: Puree thawed berries in processor. Strain through fine sieve, pressing on pulp. If necessary, add reserved berry juice so puree measures 1 cup. Transfer ¼ cup puree to small bowl. Sprinkle gelatin over. Let stand 5 minutes to soften. Bring remaining puree and sugar to boil in heavy medium saucepan, stirring until sugar dissolves. Remove from heat. Add gelatin and stir until dissolved. Let stand until cool but not set, stirring frequently. Beat cream until peaks form. Fold ¼ of cream into strawberry mixture to lighten; fold in remaining cream.

To assemble: Using cardboard, form only the sides of a 6-inch square mold with 3-inch-high sides. Line with foil. Place on foil-covered 6-inch cardboard square. Cut four 6-inch squares from génoise. Place 1 in mold. Brush lightly with syrup. Spread 2 cups mousse over. Top with another génoise layer, pressing gently. Brush lightly with syrup. Spread with 2 cups mousse. Top with another génoise layer. Brush lightly with syrup. Spread with 1½ cups mousse. Top with last génoise layer, pressing gently. Spread remaining mousse over top. Refrigerate until set, at least 30 minutes. *(Can be prepared 1 day ahead to this point.)*

Remove sides of mold from dessert. Arrange berries atop cake. Brush with melted currant jelly. Refrigerate until set. Serve well chilled.

Strawberry Carousel

8 to 10 servings

¼ cup sifted cake flour
¼ teaspoon baking powder
4 teaspoons milk
2 teaspoons unsalted butter
¼ cup sugar
1 egg
1 egg yolk

½ cup strawberry preserves
2 tablespoons kirsch
2 pints strawberries, hulled
White Chocolate Mousse
(see page 111)

2 tablespoons minced pistachios

Preheat oven to 400°F. Line bottom of 8-inch-diameter cake pan with parchment or waxed paper. Resift flour with baking powder twice. Heat milk with butter in small saucepan until butter melts. Keep hot over low heat; do not simmer. Combine sugar, egg and yolk in bowl of electric mixer. Set bowl over pan of hot (not simmering) water over low heat. Whisk until sugar dissolves and mixture is warm to touch. Transfer bowl to mixer and beat until mixture is cool, tripled in volume and consistency of whipped cream. Sift flour over batter. Gently fold in. Gradually fold in hot milk until just incorporated. Spread batter in prepared pan. Bake until cake is brown and springy to touch, 10 to 12 minutes. Let cake cool in pan.

Transfer cake to 8-inch springform pan, discarding parchment. Melt preserves in small saucepan over low heat. Strain; return to pan. Mix in kirsch. Brush half over cake. Halve enough berries through stem ends to line sides of pan. Arrange around top of cake, points up and cut sides against pan. Top cake with remaining whole berries, pointed ends up. Pour mousse over berries, spreading to touch sides of pan and filling in any spaces. Smooth top even with pan. Run serrated knife across top to ripple surface. Refrigerate for at least 3 hours. *(Can be prepared 1 day ahead.)*

Wrap sides of pan in hot wet towel for 10 seconds. Remove pan sides. Smooth edge of dessert with metal spatula. Re-warm remaining preserves. Brush on sides of cake and exposed surface of berries. Press pistachios against cake. Chill at least 30 minutes. *(Can be prepared 4 hours ahead.)* Let stand at room temperature 15 minutes before serving.

White Christmas Mousse Torte

The sponge cake base can be prepared one week ahead of time. The torte is assembled in its mold one day ahead.

8 servings

Cranberry-Raspberry Puree
1¾ cups cranberries
6 tablespoons sugar
¼ cup raspberry preserves

Butter Sponge Cake
¾ cup sifted cake flour
1 teaspoon baking powder
¼ cup milk
2 tablespoons (¼ stick) unsalted butter, cut into small pieces

¾ cup sugar
3 eggs, room temperature
3 egg yolks, room temperature

White Chocolate Mousse*

½ cup apricot preserves
3 tablespoons minced unsalted pistachios

For puree: Combine cranberries and sugar in heavy small saucepan. Cover and bring to simmer over low heat. Uncover, increase heat to medium and stir until half of berries burst, about 3 minutes. Mix in preserves. Press mixture through medium-fine disc of food mill, discarding pulp and seeds. Cool.

For cake: Preheat oven to 400°F. Line 11x17-inch baking pan with parchment or waxed paper. Sift flour with baking powder twice. Heat milk and butter in small saucepan until butter melts. Keep warm over low heat; do not let simmer. Combine sugar, eggs and yolks in bowl of electric mixer. Set bowl over saucepan of hot (not simmering) water over low heat. Whisk until sugar dissolves and mixture is warm to touch. Transfer bowl to mixer and beat until mixture is cool and tripled in volume. Sift ⅓ of flour over eggs and fold in gently. Fold in remaining flour in 2 batches. Gradually pour hot milk onto batter, folding just until incorporated. Spread batter evenly in pan. Bake until cake is springy to touch, about 10 minutes. Cool completely in pan.

Invert cake onto parchment-lined baking sheet. Remove parchment from top. Invert cake again onto another sheet of parchment; remove top sheet of paper. Spread cranberry puree over cake. Roll up tightly jelly roll fashion, starting at one long side. Wrap tightly and freeze overnight. *(Can be prepared 1 week ahead.)*

Line 6-cup bombe mold or bowl with foil. Unwrap jelly roll and trim edges. Cut enough ¼-inch-thick slices to line mold. Place one slice in center of mold. Continue to line mold, arranging slices around center slice and fitting tightly so no spaces remain. Trim top jelly roll slices level with rim of mold if necessary. Return trimmings and remaining jelly roll to freezer.

Turn mousse into jelly roll-lined mold, smoothing top. Cut remaining jelly roll into ¼-inch-thick slices. Reserve enough slices to cover mousse. Dice remaining slices and trimmings; scatter over mousse. Cover completely with slices, fitting tightly. Press top of dessert with plate to compact. Cover with plastic and refrigerate overnight.

Unmold dessert onto 7-inch-diameter cardboard round; discard foil. Melt preserves in heavy small saucepan over low heat. Strain. Brush over entire dessert. Press pistachios around lower edge. *(Torte can be prepared 6 hours ahead and refrigerated.)* Serve well chilled.

*White Chocolate Mousse

Makes about 4 cups

9 ounces imported white chocolate (preferably Tobler Narcisse), finely chopped
3 tablespoons kirsch (preferably imported)

2 tablespoons water
1½ cups whipping cream

Whisk chocolate with kirsch and water in top of double boiler over hot (not simmering) water just until melted. Cool completely. Beat cream until soft peaks form. Fold cream into chocolate. Use mousse immediately.

Domino

In this delicious dessert, squares of chocolate and orange mousse alternate to form a dominolike pattern.

10 servings

Chocolate Base
¼ cup very finely ground almonds
2 tablespoons sugar
1 tablespoon plus 1¼ teaspoons sifted all purpose flour
1 tablespoon sifted unsweetened cocoa powder
6 tablespoons egg whites, room temperature
1 tablespoon sugar
¼ teaspoon cream of tartar
2 tablespoons milk
1 cup sliced almonds

Chocolate Mousse
6 tablespoons milk
5¼ ounces bittersweet (not unsweetened) or semisweet chocolate, melted
9 tablespoons unsalted butter, room temperature

9 tablespoons sugar
6 tablespoons water
¼ cup egg whites, room temperature

Orange Mousse
1 tablespoon unflavored gelatin
1¼ cups strained fresh orange juice
4 egg yolks
½ cup sugar
1 teaspoon cornstarch
2 tablespoons Grand Marnier
2 tablespoons grated orange peel

2 cups well-chilled whipping cream

¼ cup whipping cream
4 ounces bittersweet (not unsweetened) or semisweet chocolate, finely chopped

Silver dragées*

For base: Position rack in center of oven and preheat to 375°F. Place dabs of butter in corners of 18x12-inch baking sheet. Line with parchment (butter will help hold in place). Combine first 4 ingredients. Using electric mixer, beat whites, 1 tablespoon sugar and cream of tartar until stiff but not dry. Add milk and beat 30 seconds. Gently fold in ground almond mixture. Spread batter evenly on prepared pan. Sprinkle with almonds. Bake until no longer sticky to touch, 15 minutes. Cool cake with parchment on rack. *(Can be prepared 1 day ahead. Cover with parchment and chill.)*

For chocolate mousse: Bring milk to boil in small saucepan. Pour into melted chocolate and stir until cooled to room temperature. Beat chocolate mixture until lighter in color and slightly thickened, about 4 minutes. Cream butter in another bowl until light and fluffy. Whisk into chocolate until smooth. Set mixture aside.

Cook sugar and water in heavy small saucepan, swirling pan occasionally, until sugar dissolves. Increase heat and boil until thermometer registers 240°F (soft-ball stage). Meanwhile, beat whites until peaks form. Gradually add syrup and beat until meringue is cool. Fold ¼ of meringue into chocolate to lighten, then fold in remaining meringue. Spread mousse into 10x4-inch rectangular mold with 3-inch sides.** Freeze until mousse is firm, at least 3 hours.

For orange mousse: Sprinkle gelatin over ¼ cup orange juice in small bowl. Let stand 5 minutes. Set bowl in pan of simmering water and stir until gelatin dissolves. Blend yolks, sugar and cornstarch in medium bowl. Bring remaining 1 cup juice to boil in heavy medium saucepan. Strain into yolks and whisk until blended. Return to saucepan and stir over medium-low heat until custard thickens to consistency of pastry cream, about 2½ minutes; do not boil. Remove from heat. Add gelatin and stir until well blended. Whisk in Grand Marnier and grated orange peel. Stir until mixture is cool but not set.

Beat 2 cups cream until peaks form. Gently fold ¼ of cream into orange mixture to lighten, then fold in remaining cream. Spread mousse into another 10x4-inch rectangular mold with 3-inch sides.** Freeze orange mousse until firm, at least 3 hours.

To assemble: Cut two 10x4-inch rectangles out of chocolate base. Wrap chocolate mousse mold in warm, damp kitchen towel. Gently unmold onto sheet of parchment. Cut lengthwise into two 10x2-inch rectangles. Cut each crosswise into 2-inch squares, returning to freezer briefly if too soft to work. Repeat with orange mousse. Place 1 base layer in bottom of 10x4x3-inch mold, almond side up. Top with orange and chocolate mousse cubes in single layer, alternating colors and using metal spatula as aid. Top with second base layer, almond side up. Cover with remaining mousse, alternating colors. Top with parchment sheet and press gently to flatten. Refrigerate until set, at least 2 hours.

Bring ¼ cup cream to boil. Pour over chopped chocolate and stir until chocolate melts and mixture is smooth. Refrigerate until mixture is almost firm but still soft enough to pipe.

Wrap warm damp kitchen towel around mold; invert dessert onto platter. Spoon chocolate mixture into pastry bag fitted with writing tip or parchment cone with small opening. Pipe chocolate in straight lines on all edges of mousse. Then pipe in straight lines segmenting each mousse square. Place dragée at each intersection of chocolate lines. *(Can be prepared 1 day ahead and refrigerated.)*

*Small, round, silver-coated candies.

**Available from Maid of Scandinavia, 3244 Raleigh Avenue, Minneapolis, MN 55416. Forms can also be made from cardboard covered with foil. Before cutting chocolate and orange mousse and decorating dessert, simply remove cardboard sides.

L'Africain

A flavorful chocolate mousse in a delicate chocolate meringue crust.

10 servings

Chocolate Meringue
- ¾ cup powdered sugar, sifted
- ¼ cup unsweetened cocoa powder, sifted
- 4 egg whites, room temperature
- ⅔ cup sugar

Mousse
- 9 tablespoons unsalted butter, room temperature
- 3 egg yolks

- 8 ounces bittersweet (not unsweetened) or semisweet chocolate, melted and slightly cooled
- 5 egg whites, room temperature
- ¼ teaspoon cream of tartar
- ¼ cup sugar

- 3 ounces bittersweet (not unsweetened) or semisweet chocolate, coarsely chopped

For meringue: Preheat oven to 200°F. Draw 8-inch circle on one end of sheet of parchment. Place dabs of butter in corners of 2 baking sheets. Top 1 baking sheet with parchment, drawing side down. Line second with another piece of parchment. Combine powdered sugar and cocoa. Beat whites until soft peaks form. Gradually add ⅔ cup sugar, beating until stiff and shiny. Gently fold in cocoa mixture.

Spoon meringue into pastry bag fitted with ⅛-inch-diameter plain tip. Starting at center of circle, pipe meringue in ⅛-inch-thick spiral within circle, covering completely. Pipe remaining meringue in ⅛-inch-thick, ¼-inch-wide strips across width of clean area on baking sheet with circle, spacing 1 inch apart. Pipe remaining meringue in strips across width of second sheet. Bake until meringue is crisp and dry, 1½ to 2 hours. *(Can be prepared 2 days ahead. Wrap tightly and store in dry area.)*

For mousse: Beat butter with yolks until smooth. Beat in 8 ounces melted chocolate. Using clean dry beater, beat whites and cream of tartar until soft peaks form. Add sugar 1 tablespoon at a time and beat until stiff but not dry. Gently fold ¼ of whites into chocolate mixture to lighten, then fold in remaining egg whites.

To assemble: Place meringue round on 8-inch-diameter cardboard round; trim meringue to fit if necessary. Place in 8-inch springform pan. Spread mousse over meringue. Smooth surface. Chill until set, at least 45 minutes.

Wrap warm damp towel around sides of dessert; release pan sides. Smooth edges of mousse with metal spatula. Cut some of meringue strips into 1½-inch-long pieces. Gently press into side of dessert, covering completely. Cut remaining strips into 1-inch lengths. Arrange around upper edge of dessert, 1 cut end at edge and other toward center, pressing gently. Melt 3 ounces chocolate. Transfer to parchment cone with small opening. Print "L'Africain" across center of dessert. *(Can be prepared 6 hours ahead and refrigerated. Let stand at room temperature 30 minutes before serving.)*

Trianon

A tangerine mousse enclosed in thin sheets of chocolate. The liqueur used is Mandarine Napoléon, imported from France and available at liquor stores.

10 servings

Pastry Base
- ½ cup very finely ground almonds
- 4 tablespoons plus 1½ teaspoons sugar
- 3 tablespoons plus 1½ teaspoons all purpose flour
- 5 egg whites, room temperature
- ¼ teaspoon cream of tartar
- 2 tablespoons sugar
- 3 tablespoons milk
- ⅓ cup sliced almonds

Mousse
- 2 teaspoons unflavored gelatin
- 2 tablespoons tangerine liqueur
- 1½ cups tangerine marmalade
- 3 cups chilled whipping cream
- 1 11-ounce can mandarin orange segments, well drained
- 3 ounces bittersweet or semisweet chocolate, melted

For pastry: Position rack in center of oven and preheat to 375°F. Place dabs of butter in corners of 16x12-inch baking sheet. Line with parchment. Combine ground almonds, 4 tablespoons plus 1½ teaspoons sugar and flour. Beat whites with cream of tartar until soft peaks form. Add 2 tablespoons sugar and beat until stiff but not dry. Add milk and beat 30 seconds. Gently fold in almond mixture. Using metal spatula, spread batter evenly on prepared pan. Sprinkle with sliced almonds. Bake until light brown, 15 to 20 minutes. Cool completely in pan. Refrigerate while preparing mousse.

For mousse: Sprinkle gelatin over 1 tablespoon tangerine liqueur in small cup. Let soften 5 minutes. Bring marmalade to simmer in heavy saucepan. Remove from heat. Add gelatin and stir until dissolved. Cool to room temperature, stirring occasionally.

Cut two 12x3½-inch rectangles from pastry; discard parchment. Place 1 layer in bottom of 12x3½x3-inch rectangular mold with removable sides,* almond side up.

Beat cream until peaks form. Fold ¼ of cream into marmalade mixture to lighten, then fold in remaining cream. Fold in remaining tablespoon liqueur. Spoon half of mousse into mold, smoothing surface. Top with second pastry layer, almond side up. Spoon remaining mousse into mold, smoothing surface. Refrigerate at least 2 hours. *(Can be prepared 1 day ahead.)*

Drain orange segments on paper towels. Cut two 12x3½-inch strips and two 3x3½-inch strips of waxed paper. Wrap warm damp towel around mold. Remove pan sides. Drizzle 2 tablespoons chocolate down center of 12-inch waxed paper strip. Using metal spatula, spread chocolate evenly over paper. Immediately press chocolate gently against long side of mousse; do not remove paper. Repeat with second 12-inch strip. Drizzle 1 tablespoon chocolate down center of each 3-inch waxed paper strip. Spread chocolate evenly over paper. Immediately press chocolate gently against short sides of dessert; do not remove paper. Overlap mandarin segments in one row down center of mousse. Spoon remaining chocolate into parchment cone with small opening. Drizzle chocolate over oranges. Refrigerate dessert at least 30 minutes. *(Can be prepared 6 hours ahead and kept refrigerated.)* Gently peel paper from chocolate sides. Serve dessert well chilled.

*If unavailable, mold can be fashioned out of cardboard and lined with foil.

❦ *Index*

❦ Credits and Acknowledgments

The following people contributed the recipes included in this book:

Jean Anderson
Pamella Asquith
Paula Ayers
Margot Bachman
Rose Levy Beranbaum
Lena Cederham Birnbaum
Anita Borghese
Jean Brady
Sheila Branch
Laura Cadwallader
Nona Chern
Peter and Susan Coe
Shirley Collins
Pat Connell
Evelyn Cunha
Sandre Cunha
Deirdre Davis
Anita and Paul DeDomenico
Dicken's Inn, Philadelphia, Pennsylvania
Dunkelman's, Toronto, Ontario, Canada
Olivia Erschen
Joe Famularo
Helen Feingold
Helen Fletcher
Peggy Glass
Clifton Goodale
The Great Dane, Huntington, New York
Bess Greenstone
David Griffin
Sharon Guizetti
Zack Hanle
Gloria Harris
Marie Hasman
Nao Hauser
Sarah Hertfelder
Liisa Jasinski
Lynne Kasper
Bob Kasser
Kristine Kidd
Naomi Kratzer
Jerry and Lynne Lang
Faye Levy
Ivan and Nan Lyons
Abby Mandel
Linda Marino

Kathleen Martin
Michael McCarty
Michael McLaughlin
Jacqueline Higuera McMahan
Alice Medrich
Jefferson and Jinx Morgan
Louise Natenshon
Ruth Nonacs
Katie Nunes
Beatrice Ojakangas
Pat Opler
Marcy Goldman-Posluns
Stephan Pyles
E.C.K. Read
Roberta Roche
Betty Rosbottom
Richard Sax
Jimmy Schmidt
Edena Sheldon
Southern Cross, Newport, Rhode Island
Roger Souvereyns
Denise and Jerry St. Pierre
Loralee Strauss
Laurent Terrasson
Daryl Trainor
Windsor Arms Hotel, Toronto, Ontario, Canada
Alan Zeman

Additional Text was supplied by: Abby Mandel, *Adapting to the Food Processor*; Faye Levy, *Tips for Perfect Nut Cakes*.

Special thanks to:
Editorial Staff:
    Angeline Vogl
    MaryJane Bescoby
Graphics Staff:
    Bernard Rotondo
    Gloriane Harris
Rights and Permissions:
    Karen Legier
Indexer:
    Rose Grant

This Knapp Press
is a wholly owned subsidiary of
KNAPP COMMUNICATIONS CORPORATION

Composition by PTH Typographers, Los Angeles, California

This book is set in Sabon, a face designed by Jan Teischold in 1967 and based on early fonts engraved by Garamond and Granjon.